Rewriting Alberti

THE MIT PRESS Cambridge, Massachusetts London, England

Peter Eisenman

Rewriting Alberti

with Pier Vittorio Aureli,
Mario Carpo, and Daniel Sherer

Writing Architecture Series

Preface

Ever since I started teaching, in 1960, my work in architecture has involved what is called close reading. Not just reading and rereading the canonical texts in architecture but also reading and analyzing some of the critical buildings of the Western world, from the fifteenth century to the present. Close reading has also involved writing and rewriting. But this rewriting is not in the form of a revisionist history because, though I may deal with historical subjects, I am not a historian; I am an architect and a teacher. The four essays gathered in these pages are by teachers and architects who all look to history to ground their research, engaging with precedent, whether written or built, to develop their own project. This is important to state at the outset because the subject of this book, Leon Battista Alberti, regardless of his impact on how we think about or practice architecture today, is an architect in and of history.

Reading and rereading Alberti's ten-book categorical treatise *De re aedificatoria*, with its emphasis on the harmony of part-to-whole relations and proportions, it is difficult to imagine the provocative range of ideas present in the five major buildings he worked on in his lifetime. Alberti was the first architect to attempt a comprehensive theoretical treatise on architecture since Vitruvius's *De architectura libri decem* (Ten Books on Architecture), written some fifteen centuries prior and rediscovered in 1416–1417, when Alberti was barely a teenager. Vitruvius, a Roman architect who essentially wrote about Greek architecture, was more concerned with engineering and the facts of construction than with a theory of architecture. In contrast to Vitruvius, or perhaps expanding on *De architectura* in the age of humanism, Alberti presented a theory of harmony. But his buildings were something else, something that I consider an attempt, whether conscious or unconscious, to codify architectural thought on the possibility not only of the whole but also of what today can be considered the fragment. Over the centuries, most readers of Alberti have viewed his buildings as almost an afterthought to his treatise. However, two major twentieth-century developments cast a different light on both Alberti's buildings and his writings. The first development was in structural linguistics. French philosopher Jacques Derrida put forward an idea called deconstruction, the major tenet of which was that linguistic signs no longer had to be thought as having a one-to-one relationship between object (or form) and meaning. This proposition also opened up a whole new set of ideas about signs and meaning in architecture, especially in built architecture. Back in 1985, when Derrida was teaching at Yale and architecture was engaging with the philosophy of deconstruction, Columbia's Graduate School of Architecture organized a conference called "The Culture of Fragments." In *Precis* 6, which published proceedings from the event, the editors wrote: "Expanding on the idea of deconstruction as an act of affirmation not necessarily restricted to the text, the discussion shifts to the *implications of deconstruction* in the development of aesthetic models, composition, and the creation of architecture."[1] Those implications included the unstable relations between sign and signified, between motivated and unmotivated signs, and the idea of the fragment—ideas that had implications not only for making new architecture but also for rereading architecture of the past.

The second important development, or change, in how architecture is thought and manifested came about more recently with the integration of artificial intelligence into thinking about how architecture is realized and the possibilities for signification. AI introduced new models and data into the algorithms of architecture, which in turn brought a need for new architectural precedents that have been absent in thinking about architecture for almost a century. If one traces the movement of architecture from the modern to the postmodern to thc digital, it is possible to see the erasure of what was thought to be the legacy of Alberti's part-to-whole idea of harmony and its replacement by the idea of the fragment. For implicit in part-to-whole is a latent ideality, the overcoming of which was the essence of the modern. The best way to understand this idea is in the manifestation of the real, which for architecture means in form and space. In essence, the analytic architectural drawings in this book represent a "rewriting" of

Alberti's theory of architecture, a rewriting that perhaps he himself initiated in his built work.

In the more than twenty years that I conducted seminars on Renaissance architecture, the work of different architects came into and out of focus—Palladio, Giulio Romano, Serlio, Vignola. Only Alberti seemed always present. In the interest of his unique history as a writer and architect, his repeated appearances required different voices to represent and present new and different ways of reading Alberti's work, but the curricular structure of these seminars remained constant regardless of the architect: the formal analysis of buildings, done through drawing, and the reading of critical texts on built form. This structure tended to deny any monographic status to the architects or buildings studied from week to week. It also assured that, from year to year, the content of the course was keeping abreast of the latest philosophic, linguistic, or theoretical developments that could be related to architecture as seen through a wide spectrum of thought. And it gave form to Alberti, not through a comprehensive or monographic examination of his work, but through a reflection on the kind of research and teaching going on in disciplines related to architecture today. Over the years, architects and scholars like those whose work is included in this book have related Alberti to directions in both historical and current thinking. Thus, Pier Vittorio Aureli and Mario Carpo, who both graduated as architects, present two different viewpoints—and different from my own interest in Alberti—in their contributions: Carpo on Alberti's introduction of the "author architect" and notation; Aureli on the concept of "project" in Alberti. And historian Daniel Sherer takes up critic Manfredo Tafuri's discourse on Alberti. For Sherer, Tafuri reframes Alberti in such a way as to question Alberti's role in humanist representation. This reframing is essentially what both Aureli and Carpo also do: Aureli by attempting to define in Alberti's terms the idea of "project," which he says forever changed the social and political aspects of the processes of architecture in the restructuring of society; and Carpo by posing a new theoretical construct, revolutionary in context, with ideas about authorship in architecture by introducing a notational paradigm that says "they can only build what they can notate." The analytic diagrams in this book are another form of such notation, one that offers new readings of Alberti's architecture—that is, of his buildings as opposed to his theoretical texts.

My own work on Alberti comes out of an idea of the formal that has undergirded my writing and building since I submitted my dissertation, "The Formal Basis of Modern Architecture," at the University of Cambridge in June 1963. By the time a facsimile of the dissertation was published in 2006, this work—a series of analytic drawings and a text—had long been superseded and its theoretical underpinning outdated. Over the years, Alberti, for one, has played an evolutionary role in my thinking about the formal, but less because of his treatise than because of his five important buildings. My repeat visits to and reading of Alberti's Palazzo Rucellai in Florence became a focus of my continuing work on the architectural sign, which had begun as early as 1969 with my House II project. Not until my later readings of deconstruction, in the 1980s, specifically Derrida's idea of the free play of signs and objects, was I able to formulate a more general idea of what I call an unmotivated sign in architecture. It was the important idea of free play that led me back, through deconstruction, to marking the free play of redundant signs in the Palazzo Rucellai. This marking opened up the possibility of other current linguistic concerns coming from deconstruction, such as the idea of the fragment, which held the possibility of moving away from the idealizing inherent in Alberti's concept of part-to-whole harmony and toward a more dialectical notion of the fragment as a postmodern condition.

While Alberti is seen as having influenced the status of the architect as author to this day, it is necessary to update thinking about his work for several reasons. First is Joseph Rykwert, Neil Leach, and Robert Tavernor's 1988 translation of *De re aedificatoria* as *On the Art of Building in Ten Books*; second, and more important, is the poststructuralist work on the relationship of objects to signs and meaning, which often places any work in a new context. Lastly, the analytic drawings of Alberti's buildings that students have made over the course of many years have helped to open up those latent dialogues and place Alberti at the center of current architectural thinking.

My particular argument is an attempt to show the formal issues in each of Alberti's buildings beyond basic function, structure, meaning, and aesthetics. The forty-nine analytic diagrams here are a different way of articulating the formal ideas beyond image and proportional aesthetics. The work is new in the sense that it is a reading of Alberti as a series of formal notations as opposed to the quite literal notations that Carpo discusses.

To propose a dialectic of motivated and unmotivated signs in Alberti's buildings requires us to, in a sense, rewrite Alberti; hence the title of this volume. It is not clear that Alberti was consciously developing a system of signs in his built work, especially not signs that today we can see as often countermanding his idea of part-to-whole harmony. But when a part can be seen as a fragment, it relates less to the idea of a harmonious "whole," because the fragment itself is both literally and conceptually something taken from something else. This idea allows us to interrogate Alberti's work, to open it up to new meanings.

Hence diagrams are often more able to uncover formal relationships than words. The diagrammatic drawings here are a record of this long period of thinking. They present a new and more up-to-date Alberti by attempting to define the nature and range of signs in architecture, and to see these signs in action in Alberti's buildings. In this analysis, Alberti's built work transforms from the ideal and the harmonic to the possibility of the fragment.

For my part, this is not just a book on Alberti. It is also a text on the possibility of analyzing five different, significant buildings by Alberti to illustrate five different analytic strategies of general theoretical—not tectonic—interest for architecture today. As in my books on Giuseppe Terragni and Andrea Palladio, if the named subjects ever thought any of the ideas I examine, it would be coincidental. And if sometimes the writing tends to suggest that they might have thought them, the suggestion is inadvertent.

Peter Eisenman

1 Re:Writing Alberti

Peter Eisenman

Probably the most radical changes in the history of architecture occurred over a period of some sixty years, from around 1450 to 1510. These changes corresponded to the shift from the dominant episteme of the theocentric to the anthropocentric. This was partially recognized in the ecclesiastical architecture of the time, in particular Filippo Brunelleschi's introduction of the idea of Greek and Roman linear perspective and the relation of a seeing subject to two new conceptions of space in the churches of San Lorenzo and Santo Spirito, both in Florence. When perspective is introduced as an active condition in a homogeneous space, it acts as a second conceptual or virtual space in real space.

While in many ways San Lorenzo and Santo Spirito were functionally similar, it was, and is, in their spatial orientation and articulation that they radically differ. There are two potential virtual dimensions that can articulate literal space in opposing ways. If the nave in both churches is the dominant axial condition and both naves are rectangular, many times longer than wide, then the subject can see literal depth and, at the same time, can be conditioned to see conceptual depth, a virtual condition that makes the columns, beams, and clerestory walls seem more widely spaced apart than they actually are. This is the case in San Lorenzo. The reverse condition is present in Santo Spirito. Here, because of the absence of the clerestory screen wall, which in San Lorenzo separates the nave from the side aisle chapels, there is a spatial continuity in the side chapel ceiling that continues across the nave to the opposite chapel ceiling This creates an actual continuity and a virtual flattening, from side chapel to side chapel, at ninety degrees across the nave. This can be read as a virtual series of compressive layers across the long axis. San Lorenzo has a virtual extension along the main axis and Santo Spirito has a compressive force seen in parallel layers across the main axis. This is the result of a perspectival conception acting upon a linear axis in two different ways. Brunelleschi made perspective possible, but he did not theorize it. Enter Leon Battista Alberti, the scholar architect who, distinct from builder architect Brunelleschi, was the first to attempt to theorize space.

Brunelleschi's implementation of monocular perspective led to two theoretical propositions: the subject/object dialectic and the virtual/real dialectic. Neither had been articulated theoretically before Alberti. The subject/object dialectic goes back at least to the time of the Greeks, but that dialectic presented the object to the subject in a conceptually different way in Greek architecture than in Roman architecture. While there were many dialectic conditions in Greek architecture, including wall/column, front/back, inside/outside, the Greeks were the first to frame subject/object in a virtual viewpoint. Scholars would argue that Greek architecture was meant to be seen at a 45-degree angle, that is, from a corner view that recedes in two directions toward a skyline or vanishing point, but the Greeks did not theorize this.

As opposed to Greek architecture, Roman architecture was conceptualized from a frontal viewpoint with depth being recorded at a central vanishing point, the front facade being the first of a series of virtual layers from the front to the back of a building. While existing buildings demonstrate these ideas, they may not have been brought to theoretical consciousness.

Before Brunelleschi and Alberti conceptualized a subject in architecture through the idea of monocular perspectival vision, there may have been spatial qualities such as centrifugal and centripetal direction in late Gothic space. But because there was no writing to bring these qualities into focus, they were assumed not to exist. When depth as an idea—that is, conceptual depth, as opposed to literal depth—arose with perspective, there needed to be a different kind of sign for this idea, one that was both narrative and potentially representational, but also nonnarrative and nonrepresentational. And because there was no theory to conceptualize columns and beams as signs, or buildings as elaborate systems of signs—that is, as linguistic phenomena—they were not considered as such. Only when Brunelleschi introduced the subject as a dialectical partner to the building as object was there a context for seeing a whole new universe of signs and dialectical possibilities in building.

Prior to the introduction of perspective, space was seen as homogeneous; now there was a second register in space: a conceptual one that created a heterogeneous condition in space and with it the idea of percept and concept, of what could be outlined and what could be thought. Within this concept of space was Alberti's idea of a harmonious relationship of part to whole, in which a wall, or any architectural element, was a part and the entire enclosure was a whole. This relationship could be seen, but other qualities of space could only be conceptualized. Given this outline, it seems only logical, if not natural, that the High Renaissance idea of organism—that is, a harmony of parts—would follow.

It was not until the full effects of Alberti's theorizing and building were fully codified in *De re aedificatoria* that what had transpired was recognized not as merely a humanist-inspired work of its time, the Renaissance, but also as the initiation of what would become the modern period in architecture. With architecture no longer dependent on or limited by the antique, Alberti theorized a dialectical structure between the real and the virtual; between real space and Brunelleschi's perspectival space. For it was Alberti's categorical treatise, though modeled after the categorical structure of Vitruvius's *De architectura*, that revealed something more potent than the Vitruvian principles of commodity, firmness, and delight. Alberti can be said to have introduced another triad, one that would challenge the conditions of architecture for the next 500 years: the terms *lineamenta*, *spatium*, and *concinnitas*, which changed the possibilities of spatial conception and its related signs.

Alberti's work also implied two different kinds of signs in architecture: a direct relationship outward to an object, for example a literal sign like a Gothic arch, and then a sign producing a parallel conceptual universe, one that worked inward to the received ideas of the discipline of architecture itself. Anytime something is conceptualized in architecture, the dialectic of the virtual and the real is in play; thus Brunelleschi's concept of perspective radically changed not only the idea of the space of architecture but also architectural signs. While theocentric iconography continued to appear in frescoes and sculptures, there was a new architectural sign that questioned the nature of the sign itself.

The first part of the theoretical framework proposed here is that from the time of Alberti, with intermittent lapses and injunctions, architecture that in retrospect can be called critical begins from the spatial dialectic first suggested in San Lorenzo and Santo Spirito. The second part of this theoretical framework is the change in the nature of the architectural sign to two possibilities: motivated and unmotivated.

The Book and the Buildings

It is often thought that Alberti's *De re aedificatoria* was a more important intellectual work than his five major buildings. However, if the buildings are looked at through five different lenses, each one can be seen as taking on a different critical role. In fact, the argument presented here suggests that Alberti's buildings can be seen as more necessary to the critical role his architecture plays in fifteenth- and sixteenth-century Italy than was his book.

One way to read Alberti's project is to place *De re aedificatoria* in contradistinction to his five major buildings so as to call attention to the potential theoretical value of the built work. This assumes that Alberti's idea of part to whole is accepted as one of the guiding principles of his treatise. To counterpose the buildings with the writing, the return of *all'antica*, or the antique, which has little relationship to the idea of part to whole, is suggested as a guiding principle for the analysis. Juxtaposing these two principles brings the buildings into a dialectical confrontation with the writing. And it is this confrontation, in our present era of fragments, that makes Alberti's work of interest today, in particular for architectural theory.

Lineamenta

If Vitruvius's triad of commodity, firmness, and delight was and is the scaffold for a potential discourse, Alberti's *lineamenta*, *spatium*, and *concinntas* suggested a whole new world of theoretical possibility that, when seen within the idea of a part-to-whole harmony, produced a sustaining architectural discourse.

Alberti begins a discussion of *lineamenta* by saying, "The whole matter of building is composed of lineaments and structure."[1] If lineaments are not structure and structure is something real, then lineaments are at first something not real, perhaps abstract or conceptual. If not real, then lineaments are those lines and angles which define and enclose the surfaces of building. Alberti acknowledges that lineaments could be understood as having nothing to do with actual materials, but rather could be conceived in the mind to be the precise and correct *outline* of a building, *outline* being the key word.[2] Here *lineamenta* comes close to the idea of *disegno* in Florentine painting, which means that the painted areas or surfaces support figures which are precisely drawn with a dominant outline. In *disegno* the bounding line implicates space as an entity that is possibly being enclosed, thus holding some idea of volume or of space as a series of planes.

When *lineamenta* is literally translated as virtual lines, or lines of the mind, it suggests both a real and a conceptual stress on space. In *lineamenta*, lines, outlines, and frames were no longer simple, platonic, solid outlines. Lines in architecture are literally built, thus in some way they determine space. They often become walls. But in Alberti, because of the theoretical stress placed on lines by the architect, there is also an emphasis on the conceptual.

Spatium

The second of Alberti's theoretical propositions is in the term *spatium*, or space, which hardly appears in architectural theory before the fifteenth century. Even Alberti's use of *spatium* does not accord with the more modern usage that would follow. Nevertheless, he has to be given credit for introducing it in *De re aedificatoria*, even though his framing of the term is not very conceptual.

For the generation rooted in the American depression of the 1930s and 1940s, Sigfried Giedion's concept of space/time in *Space, Time and Architecture* was somehow something radically new, in the manner of Einsteinian physics. Because no other book purported to theorize space and time in American architecture between 1939 and 1966, it is easy to see why Giedion had such general appeal. When Alberti used the term *spatium* it was never in conjunction with a word for time. But in a close reading of both Alberti's texts and his built works, one can see some of the first explorations of both space and time as concepts in the humanist world, particularly in his Tempio Malatestiano project at Rimini. More importantly, Alberti's use of space and time can be seen as somewhat contradictory to his mandate of a part-to-whole harmony, as also seen in the Tempio.

After Brunelleschi, space becomes an important conceptual entity for Alberti because it is now an active component of building, with a positive or negative charge and a density or a sparsity. *Spatium* becomes active through the purposeful articulation of lineaments, the lines or angles of which define the boundaries between solid and void. The idea of a charged space, for example, was one of the major characteristics of a modernist project. *Spatium* could potentially also be virtual space. The conceptual lines of enclosure, the *lineamenta*, make the space of enclosure also conceptual. Later, in the sixteenth century, it would become common for space to be described as volume or mass.

The translation of *De re aedificatoria* into English by Joseph Rykwert with Neil Leach and Robert Tavernor uses interchangeable translations for the term *spatium*: region, topos, place, area, and so on. While acknowledging that Alberti was one of the few to use the term *spatium*, albeit in a literal as opposed to a conceptual way, they refuse to admit that Alberti was concerned with any formal or conceptual issues concerning space, preferring instead to discuss proportional ratios and geometry whenever formal issues are broached.

The ideas of additive/subtractive and active/passive depend on space as initially inert and homogeneous. All valences are read in relation to a prior condition of homogeneous, uninflected space as a conceptual baseline. The capacity to activate homogeneous space is one of the aspects critical to the discipline of architecture. While it is often seen as a marker of the modern, the idea of activation transcends any one style to move toward something which is metacritical. The important issue that arises in Alberti's built work is the introduction of the *interrelatedness of time and space*. In addition, in his idea of part to whole, *spatium* can be seen as an element of time, for the whole can be seen as an implied temporal priority akin to ground, and the figure, which comes before ground, is the idea of part.

The literal interpretation of *spatium* as homogeneous uninflected, essentially neutral space also suggests that homogeneous space can be inflected, say with the introduction of a column, to produce a difference which is heterogeneous. In either case, both homogeneous and heterogeneous space are bounded by lines. These lines take many different forms in the evolution of architectural discourse. When its being is in real space, architecture is always already homogeneous. When an articulation in homogeneous space produces heterogeneous space, space also becomes conceptually active. This idea of active space joins with motivated space to produce the dialectic of motivated/unmotivated signs, which are two major conceptual issues in Alberti's built work. Thus, through the introduction of the terms *spatium* and *lineamenta*, Alberti allows for a theoretical frame that, while unspecified in the text, can be extrapolated to produce a theoretical fabric that can become the theoretical basis for any architectural thought.

The datum condition for all space is unarticulated and uninflected, a neutral condition. Surprisingly, in its containment of space architecture does not necessarily inflect space. It often remains homogeneous and neutral. But there are examples of spatial inflection that produce space with a positive or negative valence. For example, in Le Corbusier's Villa Savoye in Poissy, the volume is bounded by a surface (as opposed to a plane) that acts like a rubber band, holding the space in and giving it a sense of peripheral compression or containment. At the same time, the path of the car on the ground and then of the individual subject, who follows a torquing path up through the center of the space, causes a centrifugal motion from the ground to the roof. These two opposed readings of the interior space describe one of the critical aspects of an irresolution in the work as well as the confounding of a part-to-whole hierarchy.

Most architecture in Alberti's time does not seem, in its containment of space, to inflect it; space remains homogeneous and neutral. It is only in Alberti's buildings that the idea of space becoming conceptually active can be understood. Space becomes conceptually active when it is understood as a mass or a solid volume, or as dense or sparse. (Conceptually dense means that a particular area participates in many of the theoretical or abstract ideas of a particular project, whereas sparse is the opposite.)

Concinnitas

Probably the most active and consequently the most problematic term in *De re aedificatoria* is Alberti's idea of *concinnitas*. The term is rarely translated into English, even in the most recent translations. (It provoked Robert Tavernor, who worked on the 1988 translation to English, to do an entire dissertation at Cambridge on the term.)[3] And with all the activity surrounding its meaning, from stylistic beauty to part-to-whole, there is no significant agreement that conveys what Alberti meant. Now, after poststructuralism, there are new ways to think about part-to-whole relationships, particularly around what constitutes a part.

With *concinnitas*, which also implies a congruence or congruent relations or relations of harmony, Alberti essentially undergirded the humanist project in architecture. From the antique to natural proportions to the Vitruvian man that Leonardo would draw in 1490, *concinnitas* became a dominant theme in architectural thought, and it remains a foundation stone of most part-to-whole thinking about architecture today.

The part-to-whole idea can also refer back to Alberti, this time not to his treatise but to the built work, which does not seem to evince a part-to-whole strategy. Rather, there was little in the built work that could be described as a whole. If the whole is seen as a series of fragments rather than parts, then a different idea is at work because harmony doesn't allow for fragments—meaning it doesn't allow for the incomplete. Today's discourse, for example, left over from the idealism of the modern and its postmodern reaction, is merely an attempt to model the idealism of the modern through algorithms and artificial intelligence.

In the context of part to whole today, Alberti's buildings can be analyzed differently. What was formerly a whole integer can now be seen as a part or, more accurately, a fragment.

The universalizing sense of absolute beauty, perhaps derived from a sense of harmony and beauty in the relation of part to whole, was probably not what Alberti meant. At the same time, *concinnitas*, when understood as congruency, sets up an internal dialectic in the architectural sign. This is elaborated as a difficult harmony, or something that does not initially look like a possible harmony.

Also proposed in the idea of *concinnitas* are two different scalar relationships. For example, in the difference between a column and a wall, or a building and a site, there can be congruency—i.e., a sameness of purpose or sensibility without a sameness of form, scale, or material. In various ways, Alberti's projects seem to be questioning that sameness of purpose. The column is a good example. If, as Alberti says, the column is ornamental, he means that while it looks like structure and seems to be structural, it is not, in and of itself, a dialectical partner with the wall. It is only when it is possible for the column to be articulated as both a structural element and the sign of structure that it opens the possibility of being something other than structural or ornamental—that is, a sign.

Alberti's *concinnitas* is also a dialectic of space and time. Time introduces the idea of the original and the secondary and the idea of reordering the actual narrative of time to one where that narrative may be reversed, so what was seen as the original project becomes secondary and produces a reordered sequence of time. This idea can be seen in two of Alberti's projects, the Tempio Malatestiana and Sant'Andrea. Of the three terms, *concinnitas* is the most dominant in the theoretical matrix, yet when it comes to the five buildings, this idea is countermanded as each building presents a different discourse. What brings text and building into some sort of conjunction is the new conception of the sign as an internal, or architectural, reference. This is an unmotivated sign.

Signs

Unlike Vitruvius, Alberti laid the foundation for a linguistic basis for all architecture, particularly with respect to the architectural sign. Before Alberti, architecture had a difficult time with meaning because physical elements were often merely function-related; they were not regarded as signs. An opening in a vertical plane was not necessarily a sign of anything other than a presumed need for light or air, or perhaps a view. But when the opening is seemingly too large or too small for the space of a room, or for its function as an aperture, the opening can become what is here called a sign. The opening itself has no meaning; it is not a sign. However, when its size seems unsuited for its supposed function it becomes a sign of architecture, and this has meaning for the discipline. Le Corbusier reportedly once said the same thing about a window that is too large or too small, and that when this occurs, one is in the presence of architecture.[4] What is that presence? It literally means that despite function and aesthetics architecture is also something else. That something else, I have always argued, could be considered a sign in a system of signs.

fig. 1.1 The key concept of the sign here is the idea of "looking like," which Alberti introduces in the facade of the Palazzo Rucellai. There are not two structural systems in the palazzo, but Alberti

1.1 Alberti, Palazzo Rucellai, Florence, Italy. Photo: M-i-k-e-v.

deploys the elements in a way that makes such a reading possible. This move brought about the possibility of a sign in the architecture of the mid to late fifteenth century. Thus the specific nature of the physical building became the possibility of the architectural sign, as different from signs in painting and sculpture.

Centuries later, Le Corbusier's "Five Points" explicitly told us what revolutionary architecture should look like. But save for a few exceptions, the five points have hardly ever appeared in bricks and mortar. Instead, the writing simply opened architecture's eyes to all sorts of critical possibilities. Such possibilities might lead one to look again at modernist theory to suggest new theoretical propositions that have little to do with the potential reappearance of modernist ideology. But if such a theoretical opening can be said to be an aspect of any theory, then it is possible to look back to any historical period in the same way, to open vistas previously occluded from such an animated recollection. The provocation of theory is to open up entirely new theoretical constructs found hidden in an initial postulation. Here, this is the case with Alberti.

While there is much discussion of Alberti's part-to-whole thesis, even a casual view of his major projects reveals a high level of visual dissonance with that thesis. Neil Leach, who participated in the most recent English translation of *De re aedificatoria*, even goes so far as to say, don't bother with the buildings.[5] At first glance it may seem that the buildings are unimportant, perhaps because they seem contradictory to many of Alberti's major themes in the treatise. But it is precisely this seeming dissonance that warrants investigation, for Alberti's *concinnitas*—the idea of harmony and proportion—has had a profound and continuing effect on the development of architecture to this day.

The first thing to notice about Alberti's buildings is that the elements are not just mute things but a thing plus a suggestion of something other. For example, an arch or a lintel is not just a structural element; it also refers to something in another time period. That reference can be seen as a motivated sign that is moving toward a systemic use of that reference in a system of signs. Yet architecture has no agreed-upon sign system per se. Only when there is a predetermined relationship between elements, say a column and a beam, is there a sign of structure. Signs in architecture come from formal relationships, but Alberti's reading of the

Vitruvian *firmitas* does not only mean that architecture should stand up, since all building must stand up to be considered architecture. It also means that a column must "look like" it is working as a column, that it is holding the building up. But when a column is said to be ornamental, it opens up the possibility that the column is also a sign. Thus the column, the thing itself, the "look like," plus the sign of the thing itself constitute a sign system in architecture.

This work on Alberti is first and foremost about understanding that architecture is a dual system of signs, referring both outward from architecture to forms and functions of everyday life and inward to the discipline, to signs that refer to their own condition of being, to an interiority of architecture. To manifest this duality, it is necessary to establish a relationship between the form of real things (columns, walls, facades, etc.) and the virtual space within and without these physical things.

Alberti's treatise may give the impression of an overriding rationale for architecture, but of interest now is the difference between the ideas he proposed in the text and what actually appears in his built work and its proposed designs. While the writing may be seen as a theoretical platform for the buildings, upon examination this proves not to be the case.

De re aedificatoria is probably the first response to a cultural consciousness that became known as the Renaissance, or Western humanism. Alberti revealed a series of architectural dialectics, in addition to the subject/object relationship that may have always been present but was never given conscious scrutiny. Such ideas as percept/concept deal with the consciousness of the subject, whereas part to whole required no subject. The new consciousness raised the need for more expansive theoretical frames evolving from the possibility of signs. This theoretical expansion is suggested in *De re aedificatoria*, but, more important, it can be seen in each of Alberti's buildings. It includes redundancy in Rucellai, collage in Sant'Andrea, fragments in the Tempio Malatestiano, duality in San Sebastiano, and stylistic heterogeny (the *all'antica* as new) in Santa Maria Novella. Each of these ideas introduces a new binary opposition in the built work, and from there an expanded strategy of signs. In this vein, Alberti produces another aspect of an architectural sign in Rucellai. This led to a second idea of signing, the movement from representational, narrative signs—which could be classified as motivated signs—to the possibility of unmotivated signs, which no longer required a one-to-one relationship between sign and object.

It is the possibility of a virtual dialectic about space, which in Brunelleschi was conceptualized as deep and shallow space or articulated and flat space, that animates Alberti's invocation of *spatium* in *De re aedificatoria* and leads, in his buildings, to conceptualizing both homogeneous and heterogeneous space. This is one of the reasons that Alberti returns over and over again to antiquity, not as an imitation or reproduction but as a conceptual sign signifying the new.

The new consciousness of spatial attributes led to a corresponding need for a more conceptual system of architectural signing. The idea of an expanded universe of signs, particularly a universe that will take into account the expanded condition of such themes as space, void, volume, virtual, etc., begins with Alberti's introduction of *lineamenta*, *spatium*, and *concinnitas*, which also triggers an entirely new possibility in the realm of signs: the possibility of their becoming unmotivated; that is, of having no one-to-one relationship between sign and object.

Today, much of what Alberti wrote animates, on some level, thinking on contemporary architecture. It is widely accepted that his limited use of the term *spatium* was considered standard in writings on architecture, from the first century to the fifteenth century.

For Alberti, as for most architects of that time, the idea of space did not seem to be theoretically important. In fact, when writing about part-to-whole relationships, Alberti was referring to solid materials, to stone, brick, wood, etc., and how they were put together as columns, walls, and beams.

Time

The very idea of part to whole conceives of the whole as original and the part as secondary; this is a temporal idea. With the idea that the whole also contains the possibility of the part, the temporal hierarchy is removed; thus time is in play as both original and secondary, two different concepts of time that can be seen in the Tempio and Rucellai.

The reconstruction diagram of the nave columns in the thirteenth-century Gothic church in Rimini now known as the Tempio Malatestiano can be called a writing in the sense that it depends on prior knowledge not obviously available or knowable in the existing physical facts. When the fifteenth-century Alberti project becomes an "original," the primacy of the Gothic church is put into question. This idea allows each of Alberti's buildings to be read differently from previous assessments, which have attempted to relate the built work to his *concinnitas* argument. The need to relate those projects to a part-to-whole mandate radically shifts to a new idea of Alberti's production that is unhooked from his part-to-whole rubric.

Rudolf Wittkower's 1940 article "Alberti's Approach to Antiquity in Architecture" is probably still the best introduction to Alberti's theoretical work, in part due to Wittkower's diagrams illustrating Alberti's definition of the difference between a column and a pillar. In describing the two diagrams Wittkower writes, fig. 1.2 "The first motive is based on the functional meaning of the column, the second on the cohesion and unity of the wall."[6]

From this one would certainly say that one presumes the unity of the wall, while the integrity of the pillar as opposed to a wall is clearly in play. But in Wittkower's lexicon there is a further difference between a column and a pillar. He says that a pilaster is a decoration on a wall. However, we know that pilasters in the high Gothic were usually material added to a column (or pillar, as the case may be). Whether the pilaster was ever structural was never clear. In the matter of the column as ornament or decoration, however, some other reading is possible. Instead of decoration, a pilaster could be a sign of the absence of a column. In Alberti's work, this can be seen as a system of internal signs, a system that begins with a column in the round, fully figural to a pilaster, then flat to the outline of a column inscribed in a wall, to just a plain wall. This places the column in a clear dialectic with the wall as both structure and sign. The column as a sign as opposed to decoration makes more sense when Alberti's part-to-whole dialectic is considered.

One of the most active propositions to come out of *De re aedificatoria* is the idea that a column is basically an ornament or the articulation of the residue of a wall. Where Vitruvius's treatise was essentially a paean to Greek architecture, Alberti's is essentially a

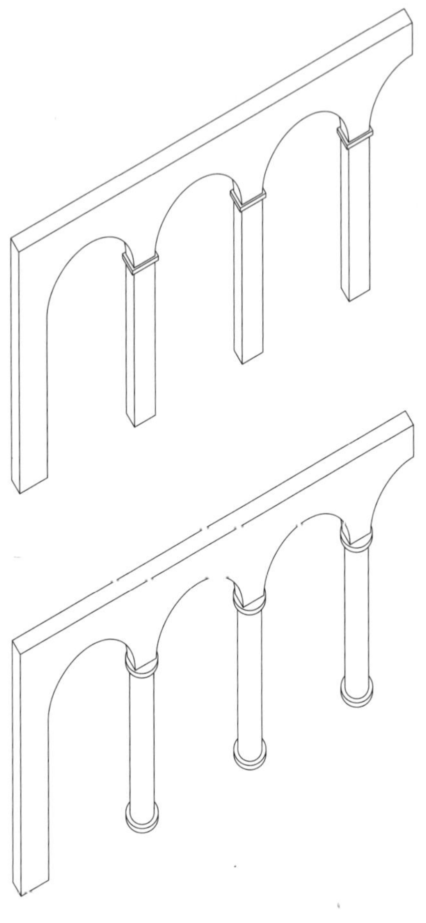

1.2 Pillar and arch, column and arch. Redrawn from Rudolf Wittkower, *Architectural Principles in the Age of Humanism*, 1949.

proposition about Romanity. And if Greek architecture was basically columnar, then it would follow that Roman architecture was about the wall. While it is possible to suggest this classification, it does not necessarily produce Alberti's stunning pronouncement that the column is essentially an ornament. This can also be seen in the facades of three of his buildings: Palazzo Rucellai, San Sebastiano, and Sant'Andrea. In his writing Alberti is careful to distinguish between ornament and decoration and ornament and beauty, delimiting the meaning and use of the column. But the buildings are open to a more expanded view of the column and wall than even Alberti's radical insight. This is particularly true in the plans of the crypt and the main floor of San Sebastiano. When Alberti says a column is an ornament—i.e., is not purely structural—he is postulating that a column is both structure and a sign, meaning a sign of structure. In this context the column is both structural and the sign of an absent wall. As structure, the column is a motivated sign. As the sign of structure, it is an unmotivated sign.

That all architectural elements, columns, walls, and beams have a binary condition was first articulated by Alberti when he implied that any architectural element is both a thing in itself and an analogical component, a "looking like" that is its inherent sign function. This sign function, or motivated sign, usually works outward in a traditional manner; for example, "this building looks like a ship." This is what Robert Venturi was referring to when he called certain buildings ducks as opposed to decorated sheds. But as traditional signs refer outward to an object, architectural signs can also refer inward, becoming what is being called here an unmotivated sign.

Architectural Signs

The new and expanded spatial conceptions in Renaissance architecture required a whole new range of signing possibilities. If the predominance of signs for homogeneous space was essentially motivated, now a virtual or internal system of essentially unmotivated signs was needed. Existing signs were referential, narrative, and essentially semantic, or what are here called motivated signs. The new world was conceptual, raising the need for unmotivated signs.

Before 1450, there was little thought given to the expansion of thinking about the phenomenal world. Clearly there was always perspectival space, but it was rarely conceptualized as such. The duality of literal and conceptual space in Brunelleschi suggests different ways of parsing Alberti's work. For this author, this includes the idea of unmotivated signs in architecture, which became active because of Derrida's work in deconstruction. For example, a rose window in a Gothic cathedral was not so much a sign of something as it was an iconic use of a functioning artifact that let light into the nave of a major church. Descending from the Roman oculus, the rose window is a useful example for describing the transition from an object to a functioning religious object to an analogous condition to a linguistic sign. Clearly all the features of a rose window had meaning in its context. It was round as opposed to an ordinary square or rectangular window; it was large as opposed to small, unitary as opposed to multiple, but it was not an example of what were to become referential signs in architecture. It did not refer to an object or a context. In this sense, it was a sign of a cathedral.

If all signs are motivated, then new meanings are not possible. The fifteenth century was a time of necessary new meanings, but for these new meanings to become active, one needed to open up a new realm of signs. This is the potential of the unmotivated sign.

The introduction of the monocular subject through perspective had the effect of creating a subject/object dialectic which changed the nature of the experience of the being of architecture from largely unconscious to a more conscious role of architectural signs. When the human subject becomes an active participant with the architectural object, an entirely different relationship of the subject to space is proposed. The subject was not explicitly stated as such, but with the dialectical pairing of Brunelleschi's San Lorenzo and Santo Spirito, space was no longer homogeneous. The former introduced a perspectival lengthening along the dom-
fig. 1.3 inant axis, while the latter exhibited a conceptual cross-graining
fig. 1.4 across the long axis.

This is a signature of Brunelleschi (though it remains overshadowed to this day by his feat of engineering with the dome for the Duomo). Once perspectival space is conceptualized and

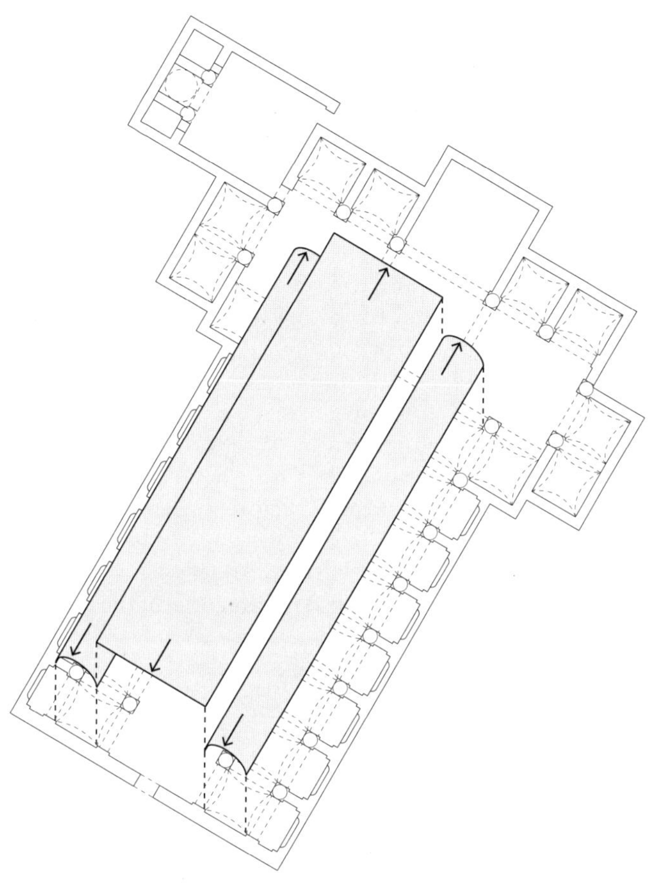

1.3 Perspectival lengthening along the dominant axis in Filippo Brunelleschi's Basilica di San Lorenzo, Florence, Italy.

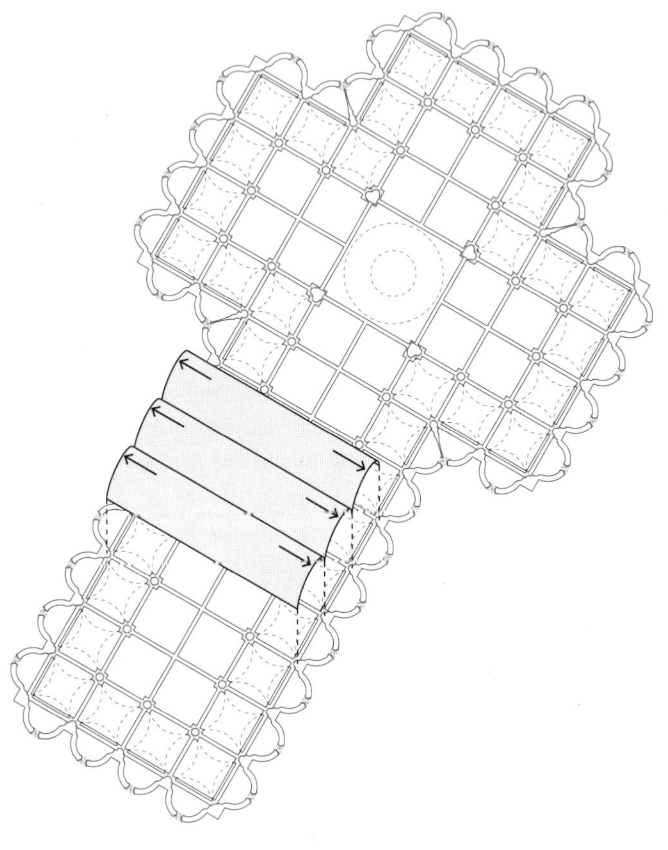

1.4 Conceptual cross-graining in Filippo Brunelleschi's Basilica di Santo Spirito, Florence, Italy.

designed in real space, the human subject is able to see real space and conceptual space at the same time. This raised the need for several different kinds of signs related to Alberti's idea of *concinnitas*. Harmony or congruency became articulated as a part-to-whole dialectical construct that, one could argue, has formed the basis of the theoretical understanding of the object to this day.

Alberti did not consciously articulate a sign system in *De re aedificatoria*, but there is no question that he put forward in his buildings a sign system for architecture that is both entirely within the discipline and, with what can be seen through a fifteenth-century lens, dialectically based.

Unlike linguistic signs, which are very precise, architectural signs are more like analogies. An unmotivated sign, which has no one-to-one referent, is more resistant to commodification and consumption because it is more difficult to read. Often it does not follow traditional sign/signified relationships. Its relationships are grammatical and therefore more abstract.

An unmotivated sign refers inward to a quality of the discipline of architecture, such as flat space, deep space, etc. Literal space can be deep or shallow, but flat space is a conceptual idea inherent in the possibility of the discipline of architecture. The eye first sees the literal dimensions of a space and then the conceptual dimension. Conceptual aspects can be marked by a solid (a column or wall) interrupting the continuity of a void. These solid interruptions are more than just marks in a primitive sign system (i.e., the sign or mark that creates the concept of flat or deep). Traditionally, concepts of flat or deep space are painterly ones that denote attempts to animate the actual flat space of a painted canvas with a conceptual frame. This idea is easily transported from painting to architecture.

There are several sources of meaning in architecture that can be attributed to the vertical surface. One is the formal condition of the surface. The west facade of a twelfth-century Gothic cathedral is not a sign of the Gothic, it *is* the Gothic. Conversely an eighteenth- or nineteenth-century Gothic church facade is usually the sign of a religious practice. A Gothic cathedral is literally a sign of a certain time and a certain use; it can be differentiated from other signs by what it is referring to. A church by Alberti several centuries after the Gothic period presents a second condition of meaning. A column that looks structural but is ornamental is one such condition. When there is redundancy, the column is still an object but it is also something more, a referential thing that refers both outward and back to the conceptual being of the object, i.e., to its original whole.

Santa Maria Novella

In the early Renaissance, signs rather than representations first came into being in painting in the move toward realism. These signs were the earliest traces of the subject/object dialectic. While most early evidence of the dialectic in architectural space is in Brunelleschi's two churches in Florence, it was Alberti's homage to the antique in Santa Maria Novella that began a history of the
fig. 1.5 possibility of the sign in the vertical surface.

Alberti acknowledged two types of signs, but only one is necessarily of the vertical surface: the traditional or motivated sign, which can be called a referential sign. This is also what makes the vertical surface of Alberti's Palazzo Rucellai so unique for its time, for it was an unmotivated sign referring inward rather than outward. Alberti's use of the antique in Santa Maria Novella is also important because it is one of the first inward manifestations of the sign.

In the early fifteenth century, the antique was often used as a motivated or referential sign to portray the new spirit of the time. But Alberti's use of the antique is no longer simply representational; it is now also potentially unmotivated, for it can be seen as an act of temporal disjunction without removing any potential idealization in its use.

In his essay on Alberti, Wittkower noted how most historians reading the facade of Santa Maria Novella admired it as having the stamp of Alberti's new antique style. Dating originally from the proto-renaissance of the thirteenth and fourteenth centuries, the church is certainly an outlier among Alberti's facades. Since his four churches are very different, to say that one is more different than any other, or that one can be said to be a precursor of a new style, is a difficult argument to sustain. In fact, if anything, Santa Maria Novella looks to be one of the last of the Gothic bicolor churches. Rather than a new style, as Wittkower claims, it

1.5 Alberti, Santa Maria Novella, Florence, Italy. Photo: Diego Delso.

is possible to see it as simply a different style. Unlike in his other reconstructions, what Alberti seems to have done for the “new” church is attempt an archaeological reconstruction, which, as in the Tempio Malatestiano, was frustrated by the impossibility of such a task.

The antique first hinted at in the facade of Santa Maria
Novella seems to be an overlay of two different times: the Gothic
fig. 1.6 and the antique. For example, the volutes added to the upper
facade essentially join the one-story side aisles to the two-story
fig. 1.7 nave of the original basilica typology. Normally, volutes have a
structural function beneath beams or cornices. In Santa Maria
Novella, the volutes appear to prop up or frame the upper story
of the basilica and its classical portico pediment. As they appear
here, the volutes also seem to be in a position 180 degrees reversed
fig. 1.8 from that of their original structuring position. As such, they lose
their structuring position and become an unmotivated sign. There
is also a heavy bicolored entablature which emphasizes the hori-
fig. 1.9 zontal load-bearing function of the facade. Here again the bicolor
questions the structural functioning of the facade.

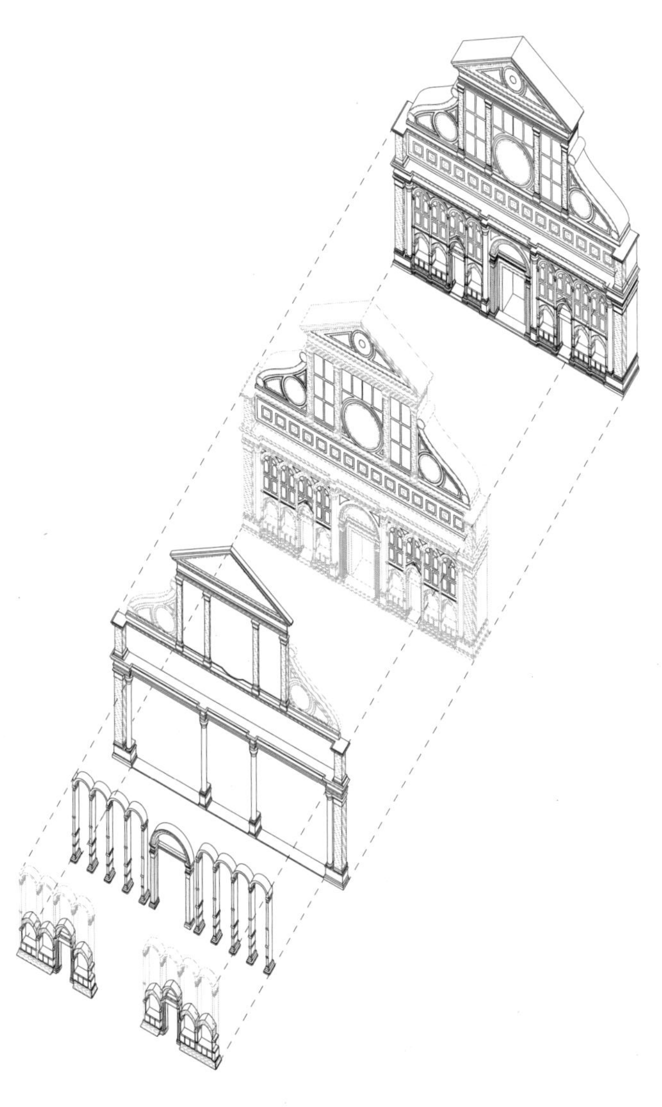

1.6 Facade elements, Santa Maria Novella.

1.7 Volutes transition from one to two stories, Santa Maria Novella.

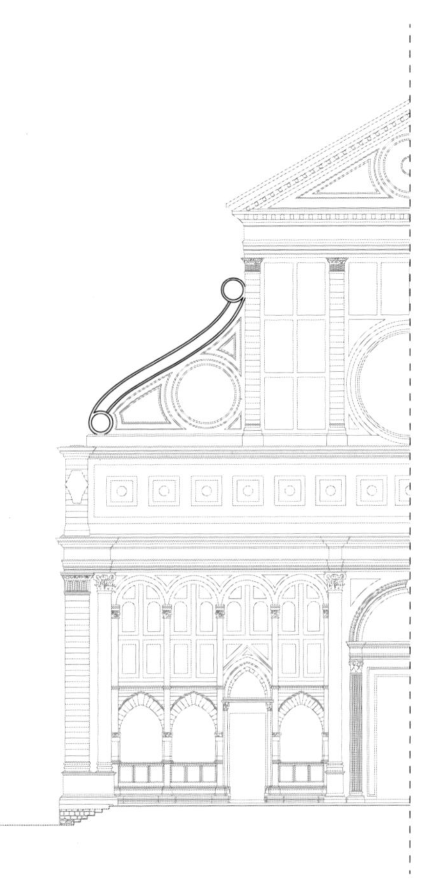

1.8 Detail of inverted volute, Santa Maria Novella.

1.9 Bicolored entablature, Santa Maria Novella.

Palazzo Rucellai

The first conscious indication of the presence of a sign is not only the traditional outward referencing of a narrative but also redundancy. Redundancy, however, required another type of sign, one that is more abstract and inwardly referencing. There are many ways to recognize an internal-referencing or unmotivated sign system. Alberti deploys two of them in the facade of Palazzo Rucellai: through the idea of redundancy and through a dialogue of complete and incomplete. Rucellai is perhaps the first, and one of the purest, examples of an unmotivated sign system.

If, as Alberti says, the column is ornamental, this means that it may look like structure and seem to be a dialectical partner with the wall, but at Rucellai he introduces another function for both the wall and the column as an internal sign function, or an unmotivated sign.

Here the column is no longer an ornament but a sign in a system of signs that includes walls and columns. The key issue for Alberti, which is ultimately his critique of Vitruvius, is the question of what the column or the wall "looks like." It must look like a structural column or a structural wall even though it may be neither. The key element in "looking like" is the presence of one or the other as a formal integer, a part in yet not part of an undecidable relation to a whole.

Unmotivated signs have little outward meaning and no straightforward reference to an external object. Rather, these signs have a disciplinary meaning, a syntactic or grammatical meaning for architecture itself. In the Palazzo Rucellai the vertical pilasters are not necessarily structural but are a sign of structure when seen with the articulated horizontal lintels of the facade, also a sign of structure. Through these two elements, the facade becomes a reticulated or gridded surface. fig. 1.10

If standing alone, the grid of pilasters and lintels would simply be read as structure, not the sign of structure, and the heavy rustication of the wall would be read as a Florentine bearing wall. fig. 1.11 However, together the two can be read as a dual sign system. For example, if only the pilasters are seen as structural, then the rustication can only be a sign, and vice versa. If the pilaster grid is read as both structural and ornamental, then the masonry is also read as the purposeful presentation of both at the same time, which is an example of redundancy. This redundancy creates a condition of a thing plus a sign, and that sign production can be marked as unmotivated, for unlike outward-reaching signs, which are narrative and representational, these signs receive their meaning internally, from the discipline of architecture.

Disciplinary Signs

Collectively, Alberti's Tempio, San Sebastiano, and Palazzo Rucellai can be seen as the introduction of something different, if not new, in the lexicon of architecture. It is not a new style or a return of ancient Rome as the antique. Such an argument would oversimplify this moment. Rather, these buildings together introduce an important question regarding the need for a different kind of signing. An unmotivated sign is technically more a grammatical or syntactic sign in that it concerns qualities which are internally active as opposed to externally related, as in a traditional narrative sign. Among traditional signs are such disciplinary concerns as figure/frame, figure/ground, gridded/smooth, additive/subtractive, dense/sparse, and tension/compression. These pairs of spatial entities are understood as narrative signs, which in most cases limits them to a condition of being present. What extends these ideas further is the introduction of the idea of unmotivated signs, which do not demand an external referent or object. In various ways Alberti's buildings seem to have crystalized the need for a new kind of signing, as signs appear in different ways in each project. These signs involve a physical state of being, some of which can be seen, others of which are only implied.

A continuing and disturbing fact about historians' work on Rucellai is the insistence on the possibility that Alberti may not have been the architect, that Bernardo Rossellino might have done the work in Florence. This is based on Rossellino's Piccolomini Palace for Pius II in Pienza, which is almost an exact copy of

1.10 Columnar trabeated grid, Palazzo Rucellai.

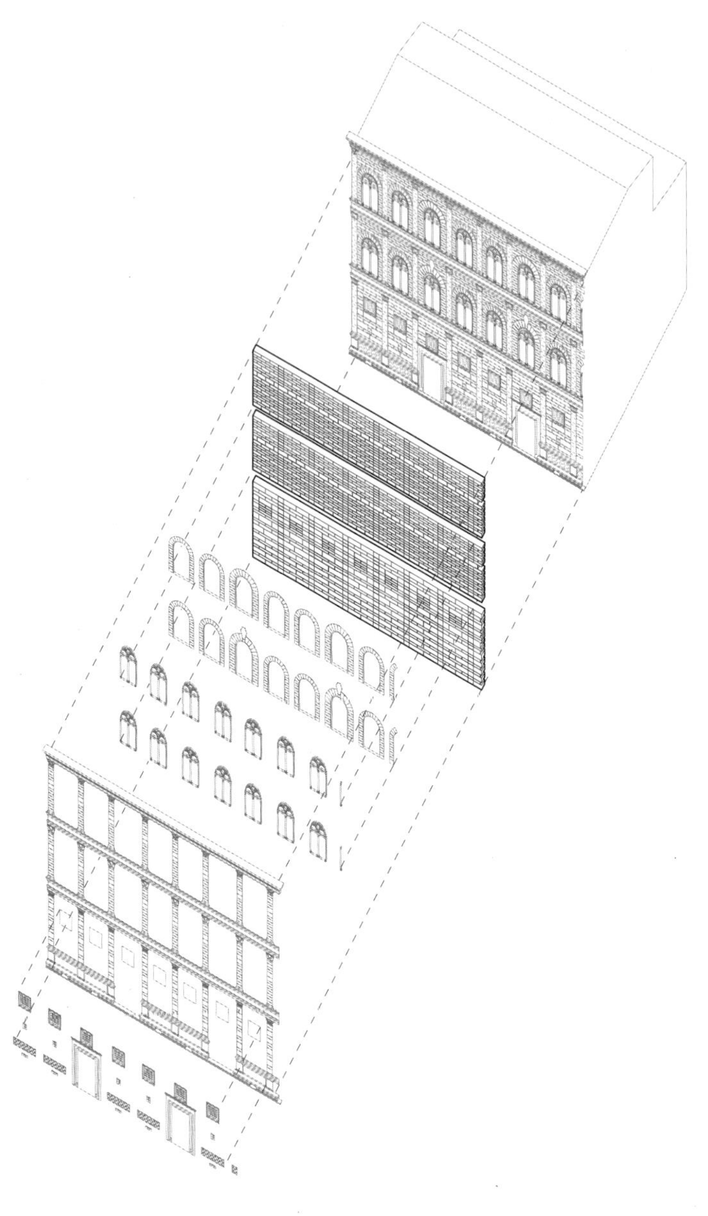

1.11 Wall-bearing system of Palazzo Rucellai.

Palazzo Rucellai. But there are obvious differences. Rucellai is a [fig. 1.12] seven-bay facade in a continuous urban wall plane, and Pienza is an eight-bay, freestanding building. The fact that the facade articulation of both buildings is almost identical requires a measure of close reading to tell them apart. It is just such a close reading that assures one that Rucellai is the work of Alberti, who can be seen as trying to produce readings that make the pilasters and horizontal lintels of almost equal value. This required the material presence to be as equal in density as possible. This is not the case at Pienza, where the grid is set slightly forward of the rustication, producing a gridded shadow line on the main gridded elements. Where Alberti's work at Rucellai depends on the minimum difference between wall bearing and trabeated elements, this is clearly not an intention at Pienza. These subtleties in the built work stand against the discourse in *De re aedificatoria*. They cannot be seen in writing.

The facade of Palazzo Ruccellai is a billboard for the unmotivated sign. At the first level, actual signs point to the incomplete nature of the right-hand edge of the facade, which to this day seems to be an unfinished reminder of three possible schemes. One possible idea is about a vertical edge that was once built straight but now shows the traces of a former segment. Another is the more complex reading of the facade as either redundancy or an absence.

The original design was probably a three-story, five-bay plan with a main entry in the central bay into an interior courtyard. [fig. 1.13] Before construction began, two bays were added to the right, turning what was an AABAA rhythm into an AABAABA with a dummy entry bay in the second B bay. But as the right edge introduces an [fig. 1.14] incomplete rhythm, the facade reveals a missing bay necessary to complete the implied symmetry.

Palazzo Rucellai is Alberti's most linguistically pure project, its internal references producing a possible condition of an unmotivated sign. First of all, the facade flies in the face of what had become the decreasing scale and size of bearing wall elements in the typical Florentine palazzo, like Palazzo Pitti. [fig. 1.15]

1.12 Bernardo Rossellino, Palazzo Piccolomini, Pienza, Italy. Photo: Pierreci.

The standard facade was three stories: ground floor, piano nobile, and attic story, with a graduated rustication from the ground to the attic story. Rucellai is a continuous trabeated grid of vertical pilasters and articulated horizontal slabs that sit tightly over an equal rustication that seems to be etched under the trabeation. This produces an overall effect of frame construction with fig. 1.16
infill panels of rustication. fig. 1.17

The unfinished condition of the rightmost edge of the seven-bay scheme leads one to suggest that at some point there had been an eight-bay scheme, and that it was partially built. A less fig. 1.18
convincing alternative is that there was no eight-bay scheme, and that what remains today on the rightmost edge is the incremental building out from the column line. It is easy to imagine what an eight-bay facade would look like, but given what exists, it is not as easy to imagine how the double entry would work. Therefore, it is possible to think that for Alberti a seven-bay scheme would produce the very temporal and physical uncertainty that was contrary to *concinnitas*. In doing so, the scheme produced an active dialectic that maintained the uncertainty central to each phase of the building project.

1.13 AABAA five-bay facade speculation, Palazzo Rucellai.

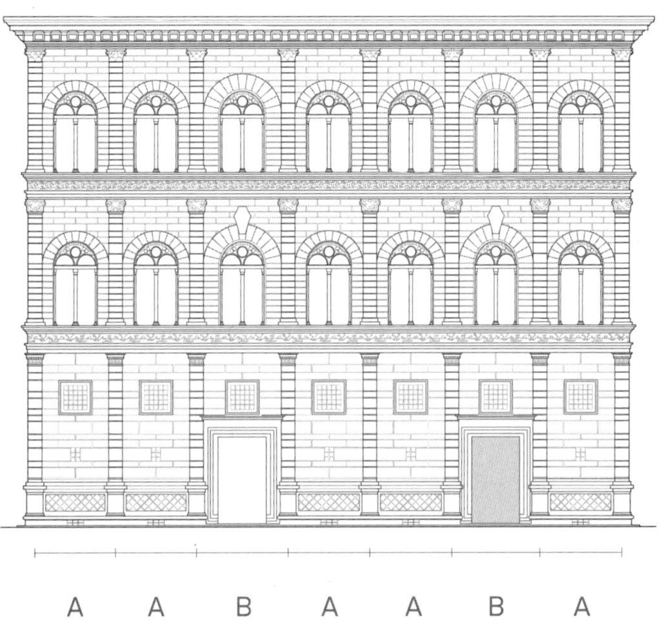

1.14 AABAABA facade rhythm with dummy door, Palazzo Rucellai.

1.15 Filippo Brunelleschi and Luca Fancelli, Palazzo Pitti, Florence, Italy. Graduated rustication of stories. Photo: Diego Delso.

1.16 Alberti, Palazzo Rucellai, Florence, Italy. Equal rustication of stories. Photo: Miguel Hermoso Cuesta.

1.17 Frame and infill rustication, Palazzo Rucellai.

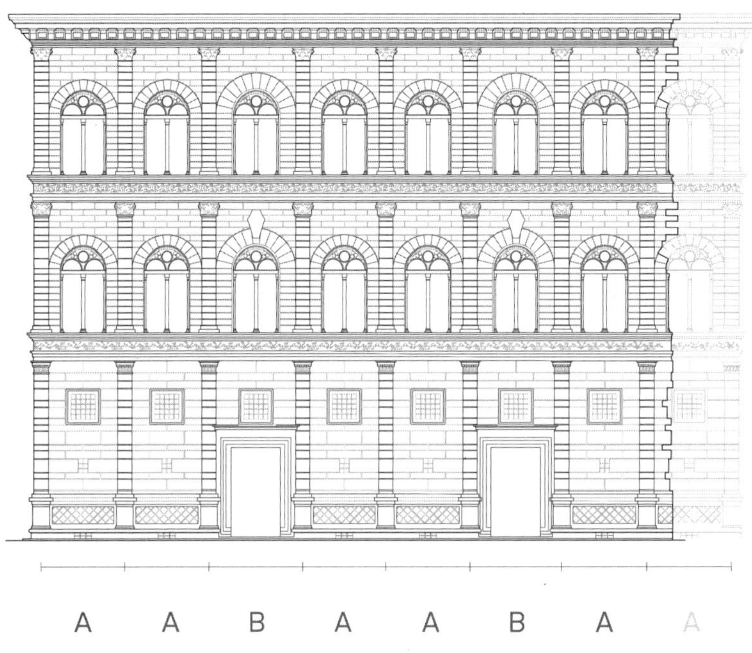

1.18 Implied symmetry of an AABAABAA rhythm and unfinished right edge, Palazzo Rucellai.

San Sebastiano

The church of San Sebastiano in Mantua, begun in 1460, presents figs. 1.19, 20 a dialectic between column and wall. The crypt, which is entered at grade, is clearly overstructured with a field of columns, while the first floor, which contains the nave, is noticeable for its absence of columns. Most other churches have some intercolumniation. Even the Roman wall churches had evidence of columns.

The sign system in San Sebastiano involves the redundancy of column and wall. The dialectic is internal, between the crypt fig. 1.21 level and the nave level. This dialogue would not be possible but for the fact that the crypt is entered at ground level and the nave at one level above; but this is not the issue. Rather, the crypt is articulated by a dense grid of oversized square columns that produce figs. 1.22, 23 a system of tightly articulated square bays. In contrast, the nave figs. 1.24–26 is a cruciform space defined by perimeter walls.

There are no columns in the nave space. If the crypt looks overstructured, the nave looks understructured. This condition means there is something present that is not structuring. This is Alberti's first use of redundancy to indicate the presence (or absence) of a sign. At San Sebastiano, there is almost no reference to a style, either Gothic or antique. Ironically, the column, which Alberti sees, in *De re aedificatoria*, as ornamental, is theoretically both overstructured and understructured. This leads to a tightly scaled space in the crypt and a single overscaled space in the nave. In San Sebastiano the column is a sign. It is the first appearance of a sign that is either a referential outward sign or an inward unmotivated, grammatical sign. Such a condition of sign can only be read in the building and not in the text.

1.19 Alberti, San Sebastiano, Mantua, Italy. Photo: Sailko.

1.20 Facade, San Sebastiano.

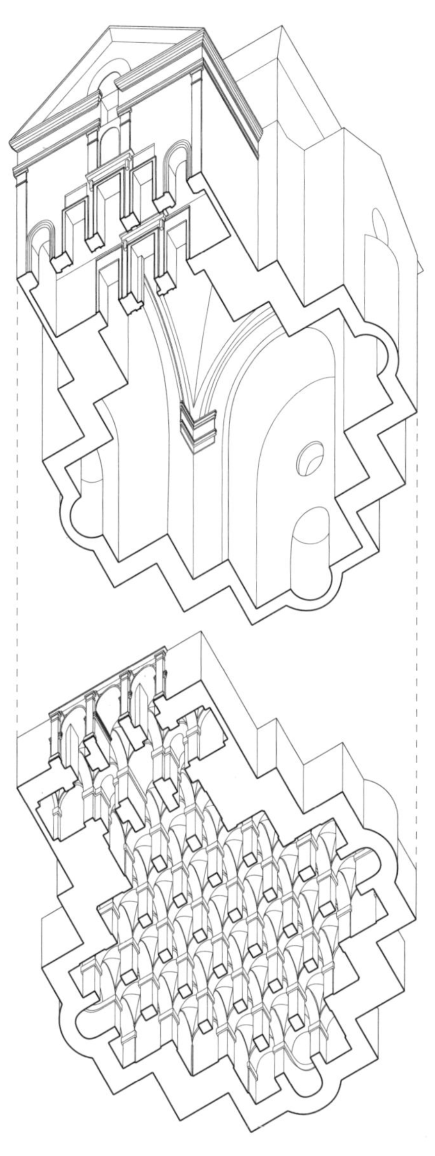

1.21 Dialectic between crypt and nave, San Sebastiano.

1.22 Plan of crypt, San Sebastiano.

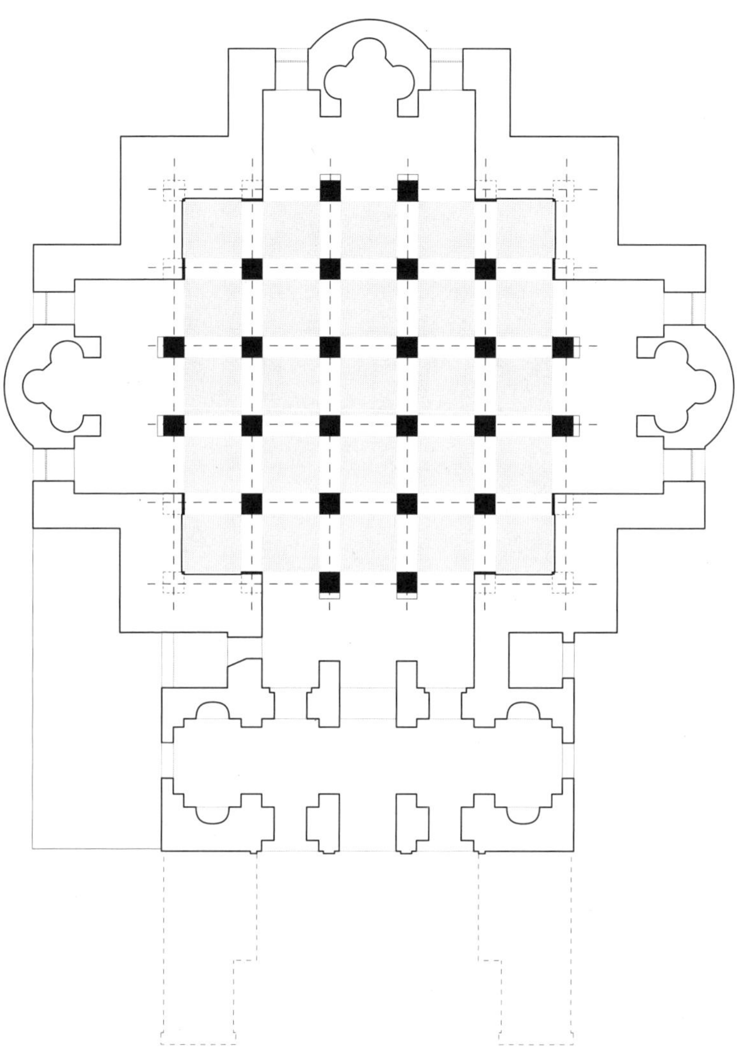

1.23 System of square bays in the crypt, San Sebastiano.

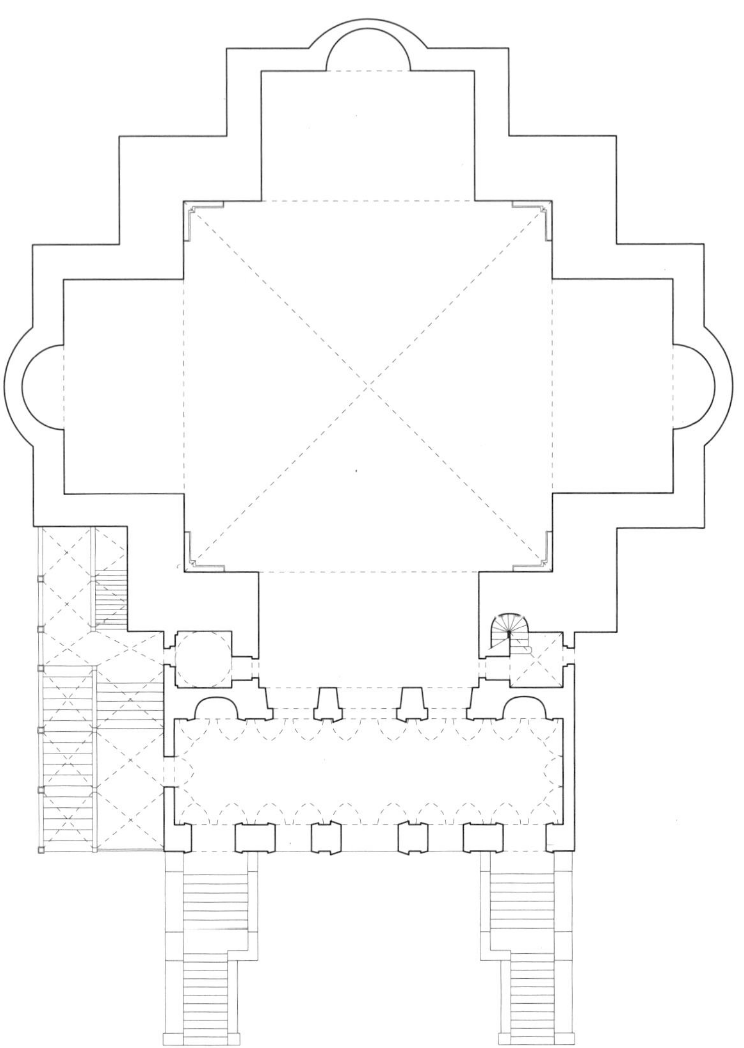

1.24 Plan of nave, San Sebastiano.

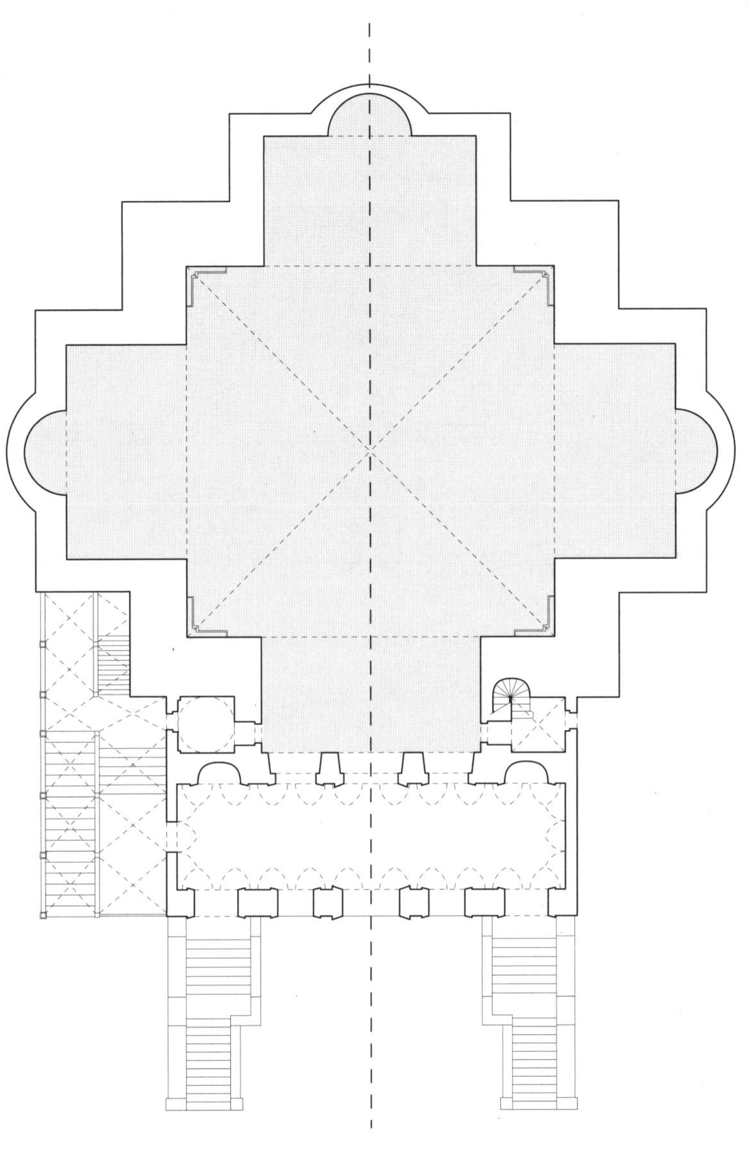

1.25 Nave formed by cruciform walls, San Sebastiano.

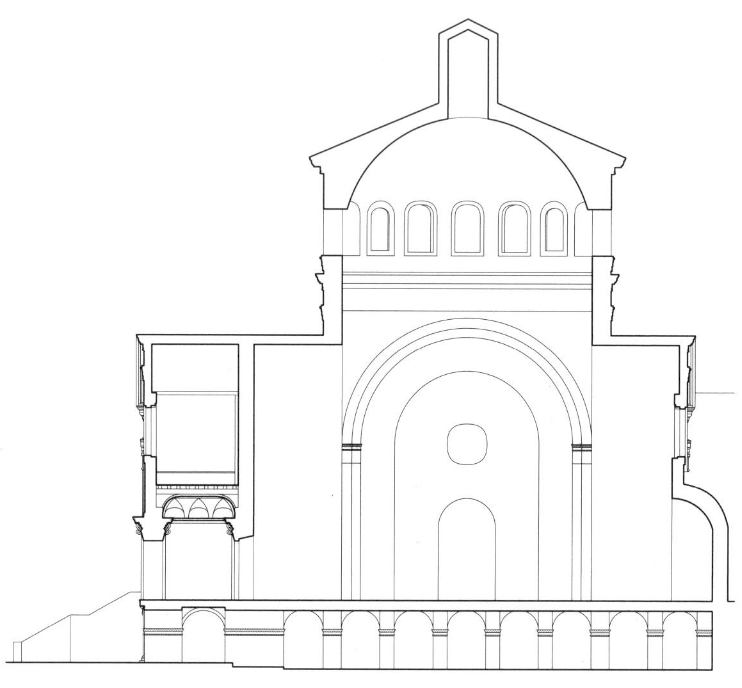

1.26 Section, San Sebastiano.

Sant'Andrea

Each of Alberti's five major building projects has some condition of a potentially unmotivated sign. At Sant'Andrea there are two different manifestations of unmotivated signs. The first is the facade, the superposition of a vernacular Greek temple front and fig. 1.27 a Roman triumphal arch in which neither trope is dominant—often an indication of an unmotivated sign.

The Greek temple front historically refers to a sacred or religious building. This is what could be called a motivated sign. fig. 1.28 Here, in a second reading, it loses its religious significance and becomes a vernacular facade, but it still exists as a motivated sign that denotes a type of building. In its iteration on the facade of Sant'Andrea, the vernacular temple front is overlaid on what was once another iconic or symbolic sign: a reading of the triumphal Arch of Trajan at Ancona without reference to it as marking the celebration of a Roman victory. The scale of the arch says Sant'An- fig. 1.29 drea is an important public building, but when overlaid on the Greek temple front the arch becomes an unmotivated sign; that is, a sign without an external symbolic meaning. Here it is merely a new source for the deployment of columns and beams. The superposition of these two disparate conventions on the vertical plane questioned the seeming historicity of the parts. fig. 1.30

With the arch, Alberti places a giant barrel vault where the ocular window is traditionally found in a church front. Inside fig. 1.31 Sant'Andrea, the scale of the column-free space is a secondary reference to the antique Basilica of Maxentius in Rome, but not an exact copy. Here, a second unmotivated sign occurs in the relation fig. 1.32 of the nave bay elevations to the front bay elevation. This is one of fig. 1.33 the few times that the bays are the same from interior to exterior. Instead of denoting the difference between the sides and front of the building, the readings of both front and interior are the same. If actual differentiation or notational differentiation is a norm in front-to-side relationships, then side-to-front sameness becomes what is being called here an unmotivated sign—that is, a sign with no external referent.

There are three different possible precedents for Sant'Andrea. Two concern the facade, and a third the internal organization of the side chapels in relation to the front facade. Sant'Andrea is

1.27 Alberti, Sant'Andrea, Mantua, Italy. Photo: Paolo Monti.

1.28 Typical Greek vernacular temple front.

an example of a church that combines the referential or motivated sign and the unmotivated sign. It is referential when it refers to the triumphal Arch of Trajan or to the Greek vernacular temple front, but when the sign refers to both elements simultaneously it becomes a superposition or a collage, which changes the sign from being merely referential to becoming a potentially unmotivated sign. This unique invocation of an unmotivated sign is even more complex here than at Tempio Malatestiano.

To understand the subtlety and the complexity of Sant'Andrea it is necessary to think in two directions: outward to something like the Arch of Trajan and inward to the possible unmotivated signs of the interior. By 1470, at which time Alberti had started all of his architectural projects, it was understood that he was using the antique style as a sign of a progressive externality and to develop a series of internal dialectical signs. Therefore, it is not surprising that in Sant'Andrea he takes two externalities and turns them into a unitary internality by superposing the Greek
fig. 1.34 temple front and a triumphal arch to produce, through collage, a new manifestation: a Roman Catholic icon forged from pagan and secular icons. A close reading of these collaged elements complicates any simple interpretation because Alberti took the columnar elements of each type and flattened them into a bas-relief wall,
fig. 1.35 making the columns into pilasters.

To do this, it was necessary to make changes in detail without losing the basic typology. One only needs to understand the difference between the entry to Sant'Andrea and the Arch of Tra-
fig. 1.36 jan to see this. Second, the temple front text has a pediment, which at Sant'Andrea is slightly compressed, while the arch is topped by
fig. 1.37 a deep entablature. The Arch of Trajan has a heavy projecting cornice that reads with the bottom chord of the entablature as a deep lintel, but no such articulation is present at Sant'Andrea. The Arch of Trajan also has two vertical recesses that accentuate the vertical
fig. 1.38 fluting of four round columns. These elements are all typologically the same at Sant'Andrea, but the columns are flattened to read as giant-order pilasters. The idea is similar to the flattened
fig. 1.39 column-wall relationship in the facade of San Sebastiano.

Alberti did not use the triumphal arch as a literal "antique" precedent. Rather, it was possible to read the triumphal arch, stripped of its columns, in a second context as a vernacular

1.29 Arch of Trajan, Ancona, Italy.

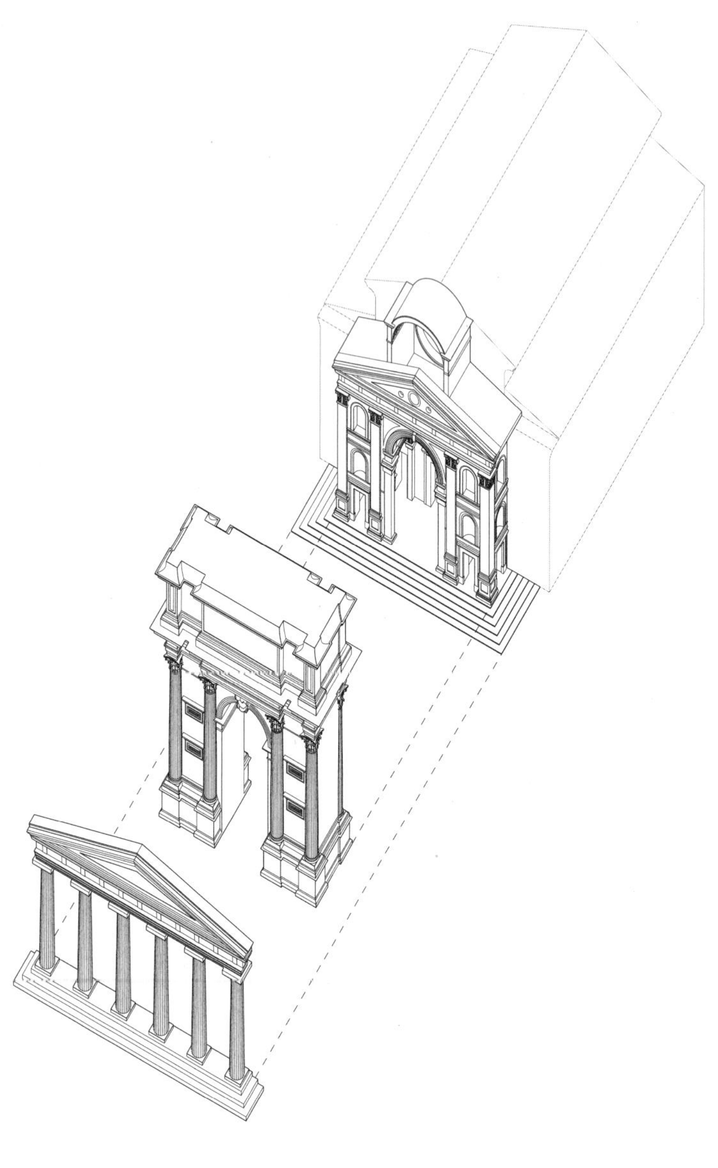

1.30 Superposition of a typical Greek temple front and a giant triumphal arch on the facade, Sant'Andrea.

1.31 Giant barrel vault arch on the facade, Sant'Andrea.

1.32 Basilica of Maxentius, Rome, Italy. Photo: Jamie Heath.

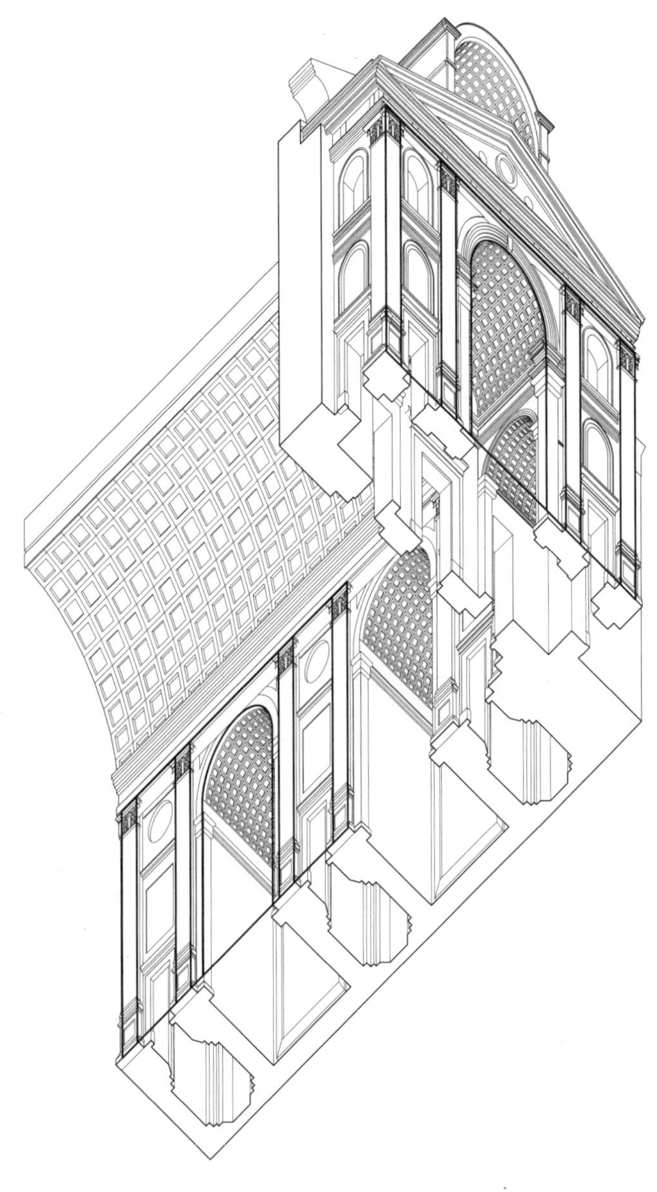

1.33 Relationship between the side chapels and the front facade, Sant'Andrea.

fig. 1.40 columnar arcade. Similarly, the Greek temple front could now be seen as interlinked with the pilasters of the triumphal arch, thus producing a second reading of the antique, not unlike the double reading of the Rucellai facade. But again, there is no consistent style from building to building, Rucellai being a quasi-rationalist exercise while Sant'Andrea was a superposition of antique motifs
fig. 1.41 coupled with a nave at the giant scale of a Roman basilica.

It is the removal of the columns of the triumphal arch that allows for this more complex reading. That this second reading is possible suggests an expanded view of harmony, as expressed in Alberti's idea of *concinnitas*. Together with the increased scale of the nave and elimination of the side aisles, Sant'Andrea suggests the distance Alberti would move away from a simple understand-
figs. 1.42, 43 ing of *concinnitas* as scalar harmony.

Fragment

One of the most important ideas at work in Alberti's buildings is that of the fragment, which countermands the part-to-whole thesis of harmony and in itself is neither a part nor a whole. If a fragment is considered a specific kind of part that represents temporal specificity, then several of Alberti's projects can be seen to inform such a contemporary discourse. A part, then, is not only a fragment of a whole; the fragment itself contains missing aspects of a whole. In this sense, it is something other than an addition, but at the same time it compensates for a lack in the original.

Here a fragment is considered both an addition to something and a substitution. It is an undecidable exteriority that is both within and without the work. It is an other that makes one aware of the nature of the whole, makes it more palpable and more conceptually clear. Many fragments are also elements that make any original more aware of its original lack. A fragment also clarifies through its positioning its difference from the whole. A fragment is also a disjunction, a dissonance, and a resistance to a whole.

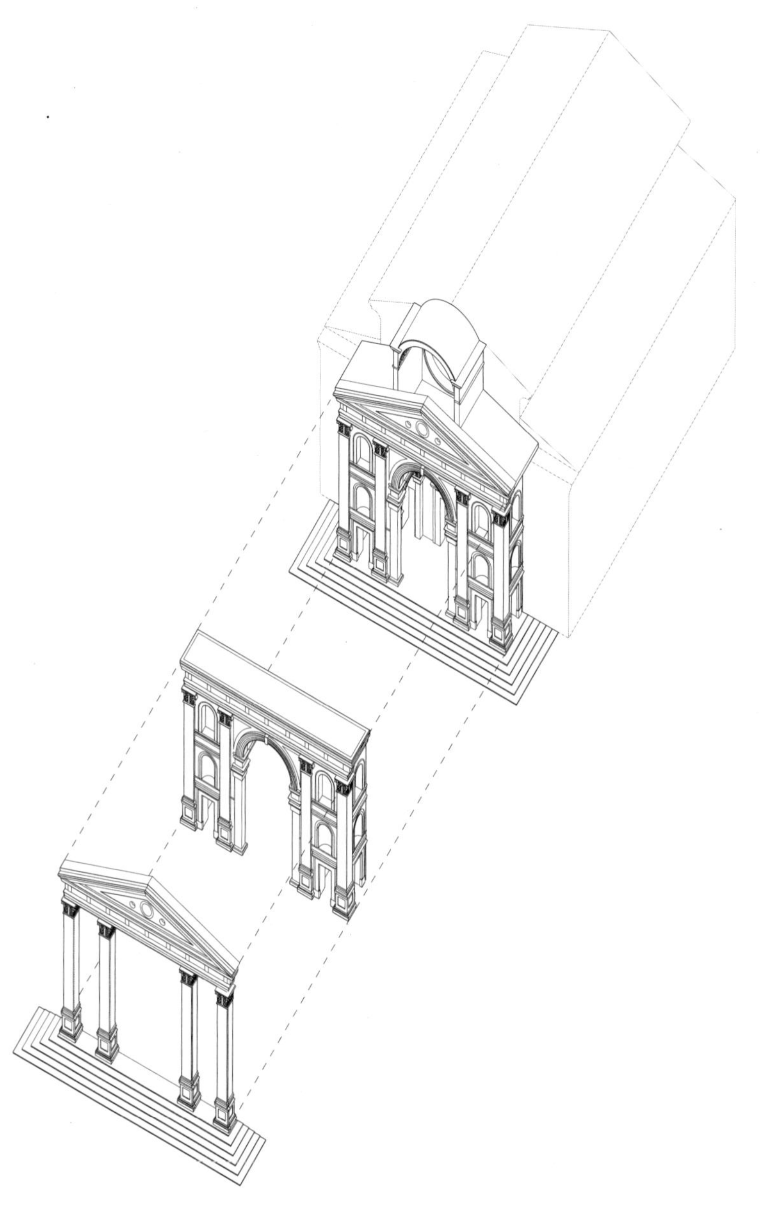

1.34 Superpositioning of temple front onto triumphal arch on the facade, Sant'Andrea.

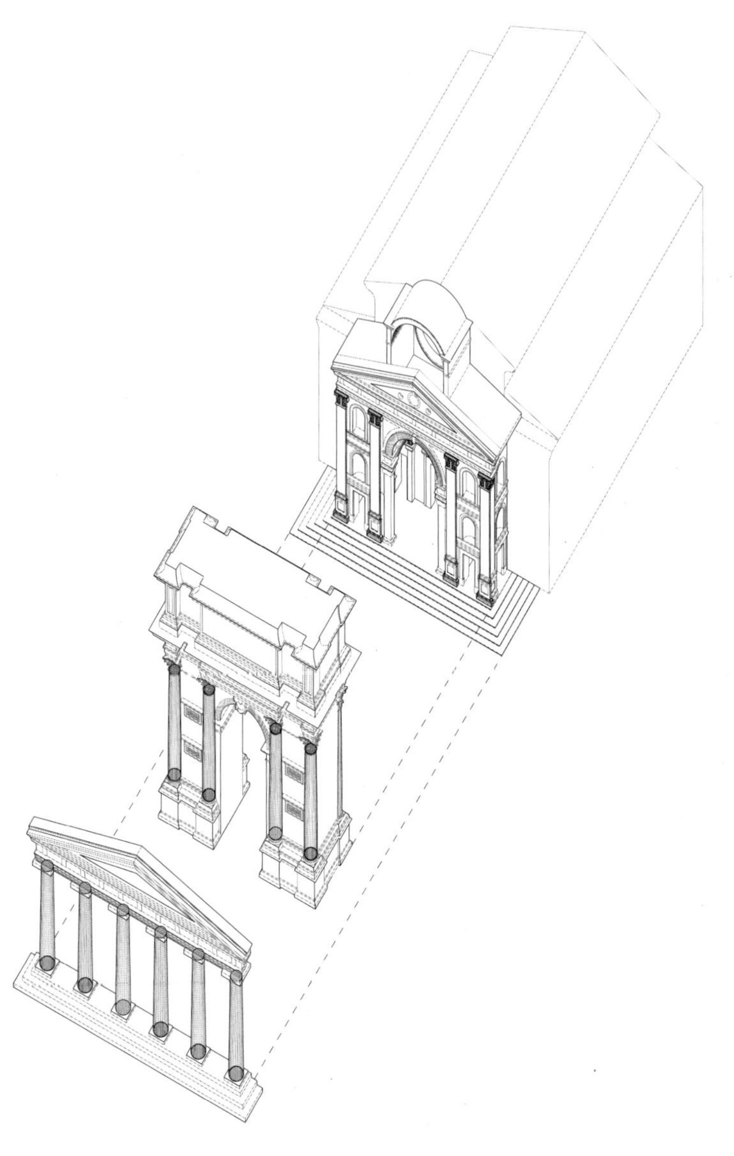

1.35 Flattening of columns into a bas-relief wall, Sant'Andrea.

1.36 Worm's-eye cut through the entry, Sant'Andrea.

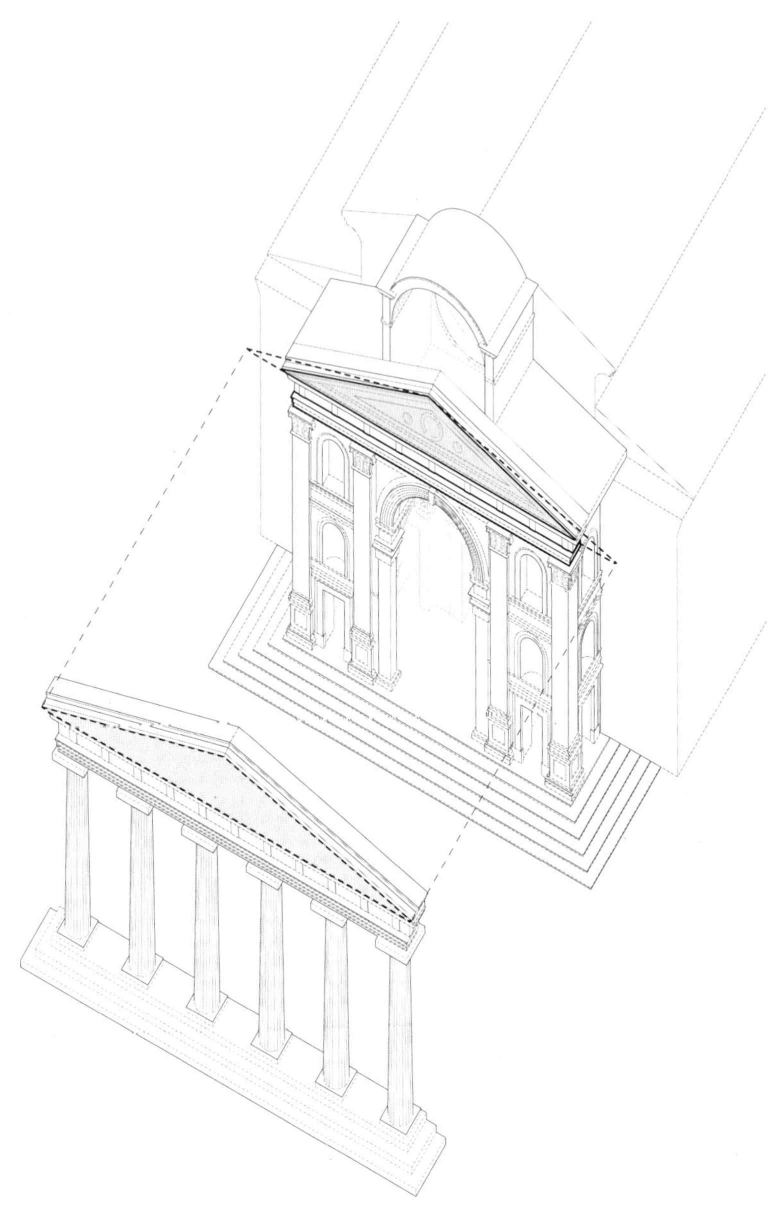

1.37 Compressed pediment and arch topped by a deep entablature, Sant'Andrea.

1.38 Vertical recesses accentuate the vertical fluting, Arch of Trajan.

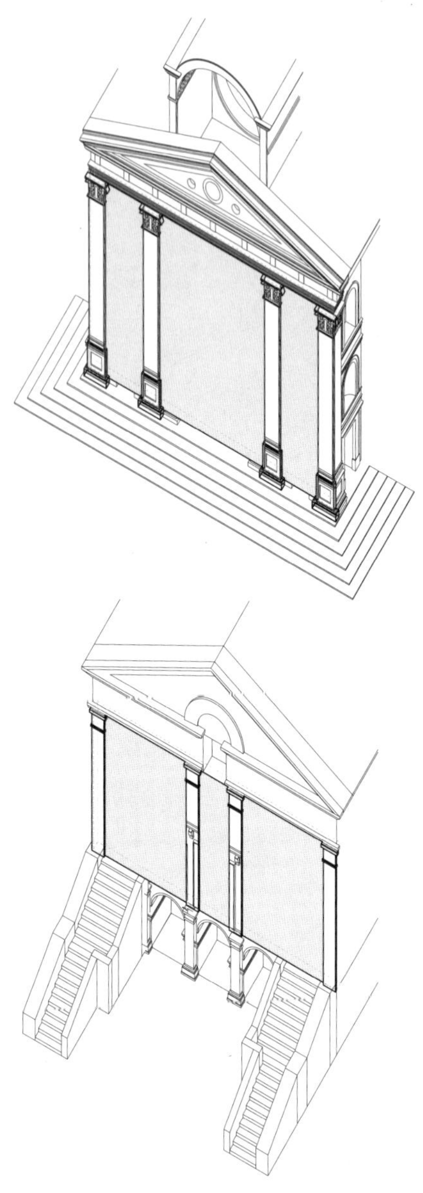

1.39 Similar treatment of column-wall relationship on the facades of San Sebastiano and Sant'Andrea.

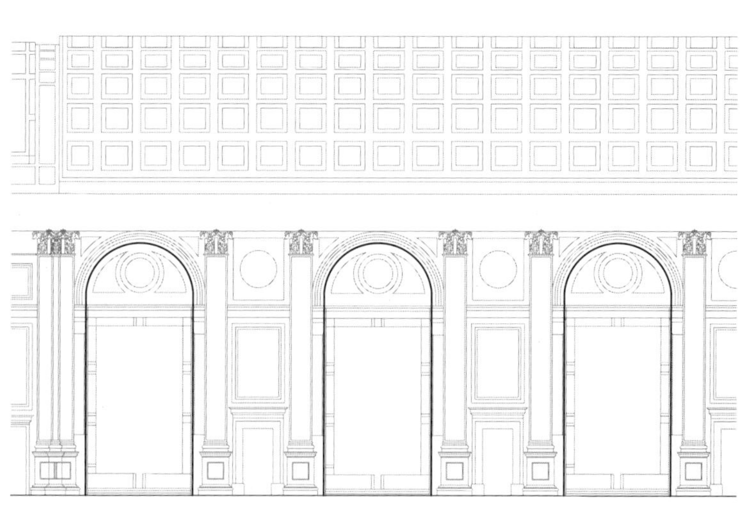

1.40 Interior elevation reads as a typical vernacular columnar arcade, Sant'Andrea.

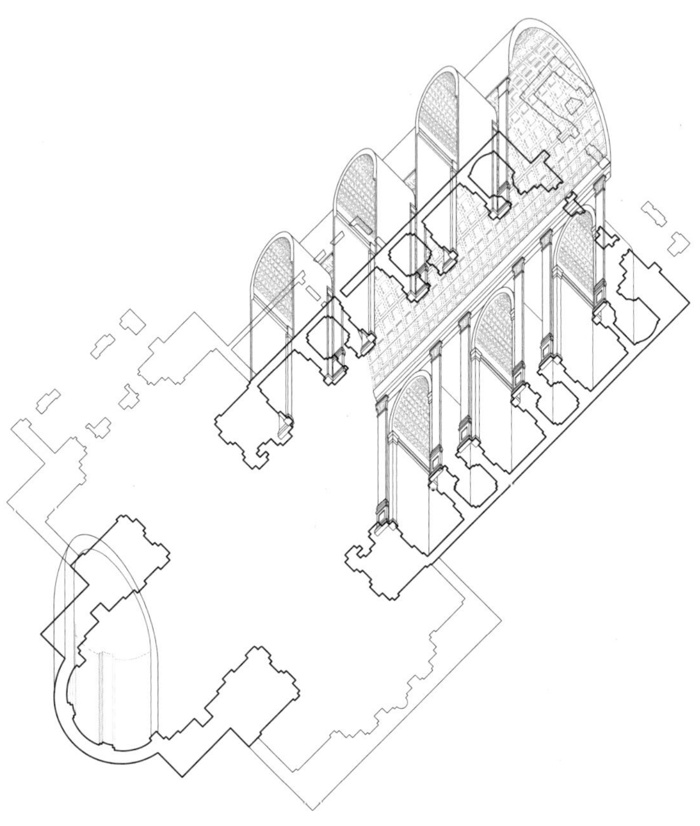

1.41 Simulation of Roman basilica, Sant'Andrea.

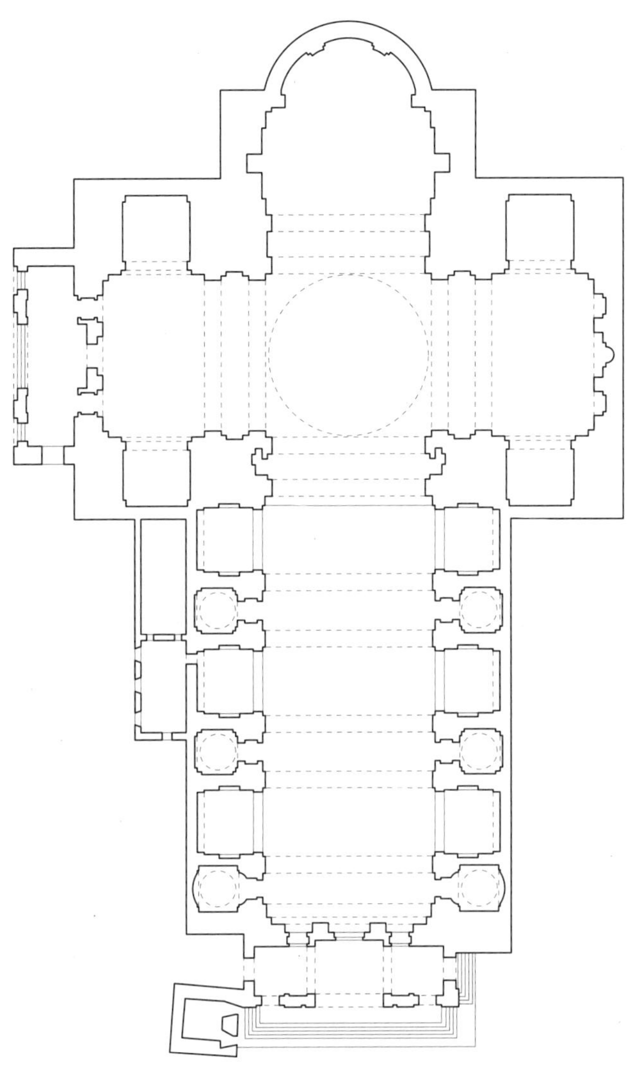

1.42 Plan, Sant'Andrea.

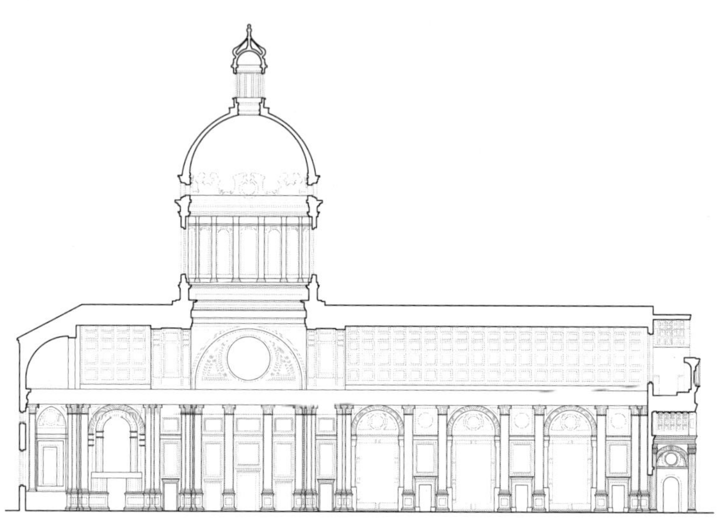

1.43 Section, Sant'Andrea.

The idea of the fragment introduces in a work not just presence but also a conceptualized absence in the dialectic literal space / void space, and an idea about that absence. A fragment is an addition with a temporal aspect in that it is always a missing part.[7] It therefore always comes after an original addition. The idea of fragment introduces, in any work, not just presence but also a conceptualized absence, a void space. Fragment in the Derridean sense conceptualizes absence, which is in the original whole in the harmony of part to whole. Now there is the actual space plus an idea about absence.

In Alberti's idea of the relationship of part to whole, the idea of the *fragment* is a more flexible concept. It allows for an indeterminacy between the original and the addition, and between part and whole. This indeterminacy removes the hierarchical implications of an original from the term *ground*, as well as the sense of an original to which a part has been added, thereby disrupting the reading of part to whole.

In order to deny, or lessen, the temporal value of the original, poststructuralist thought attempted to suggest that the term "supplement" or "fragment" be considered not just as an addition to an original but also a substitute for an original, and thus already originally part of the whole. In this context it is possible to read several fragments in Alberti's building projects that achieve a similar purpose and deny any temporal priority of the classical or ideal idea of harmony.

Thus fragment as an idea overcomes the idealizing hierarchy of part to whole. It moves two ways: toward completion or away from completion, as the idea of fragment, while it adds something, is missing something, is a part of an(other) original whole. Thus the fragment is also an absence and a substitute for presence. What Alberti does, which achieves the status of a trope, is create a condition where what was assumed to be an original is now questioned, and in doing so is no longer a whole but becomes a part. This condition is conceptually active in the Tempio Malatestiano.

Tempio Malatestiano

figs. 1.44, 45 The Tempio Malatestiano, the most complex of Alberti's building projects, involves a two-step process that produces a dialectic between old and new. In this sense there is what can be called a temporal dimension to the architectural signs. Alberti's five buildings are important because they all propose conditions in the built work that can only be understood as a temporal relationship between what exists and what existed prior to Alberti's work. In the case of the Tempio, this relationship is between the Gothic and *all'antica*.

This temporal bifurcation puts an emphasis on the imagination as opposed to the experience of the subject. The new nature of signs brings about a radical change in the subject-object relationship, from the former experience of the object/sign to the prior knowledge required to recognize signs. Where today the digital proposes the experience of being as the important condition of the object/subject sign, Alberti suggested that prior knowledge and the imagination were required to understand the dialectic implicit in this discourse.

The site of Alberti's intervention in Rimini is an existing basilica church of the thirteenth century. The Gothic church was a partial ruin that required a number of the nave columns to be rebuilt. This made the existing frame a foil for Alberti's intervention. It is often thought that the columns were rebuilt only for structural reasons. While that may be true—and there is no documentation to the contrary—it is also possible to suggest another interpretation. In order to make the maximum differentiation between the existing Gothic frame and the fifteenth-century *all'antica* intervention that Alberti proposed, it would have been important to have the Gothic original present to create an internal dialectic between the existing building and Alberti's work. A second important relationship between the Gothic structure and the fifteenth-century project entails what can be seen as the purposeful misalignment in the bay structure of Alberti's exterior wrapper with the existing bays. The misalignment also neutralizes any temporal priority between the two elements. Since no one intervention is dominant—i.e., one as the original

1.44 Alberti, Tempio Malatestiano, Rimini, Italy. Facade. Photo: Meyasu.

1.45 Elevation as intended in original design, Tempio Malatestiano.

ground and one as figure—both conditions refer internally to one another. fig. 1.46

This move questions the intention of Alberti's *concinnitas* by calling attention to a natural or possible complex harmony between the two conditions. Since the new addition at Rimini seems purposely made not to correspond with the Gothic bays in either number, scale, or alignment, it must be assumed that there is some reason for this misalignment. One possibility is in the form of an addition that contains a missing piece of a potential whole but never quite completes that whole. The possible whole is within what can be seen as a fragment.

It is assumed that Alberti intended to make it seem like the Gothic nave was intact when he proposed his classical wrapper. Wittkower pointed out that the renovation work on the Gothic bays was clearly the same as the original. However, for the argument here one has to assume that Alberti wanted a clear contrast between old and new so that he could add a stylistic and temporal dimension in line with his concept of *concinnitas*. If *concinnitas* means something like harmony or congruency, then the Tempio becomes an example of part to whole, but the relationship of the stylistic differences can also be taken to suggest both incongruity and the idea of the fragment. This duality brings the Tempio into a radically different light. In making the module of the new classical wrapper not only different but also stripped of any literal congruency with the existing grid of Gothic columns, it extends the definition of *concinnitas* beyond the harmony of simple alignment.

If Alberti's wrapper had been aligned with the original church grid, the wrapper would seem to be contiguous with the structure and therefore could be read as a continuity of structure—that is, as structuring. Instead, the new grid is read as a referential sign of antiquity as well as a fragment, which is an internal unmotivated sign.

The partial rebuilding of the thirteenth-century nave columns allowed Alberti to suggest a more complex idea of part to whole, or a more complex idea of harmony, by purposely suggesting a new order that aligns with neither the rebuilt columnar structure nor the new wrapper. Had this columnar structure not been restored, this idea of a more complex part-to-whole relation—the physical misalignment and the temporal

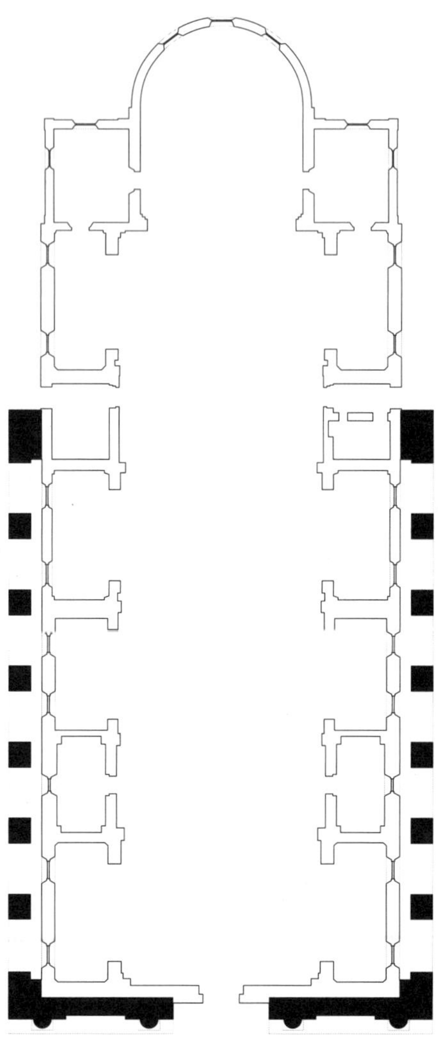

1.46 Grid of Tempio Malatestiano as ground and Alberti's wrapper as figure.

misalignment of the wrapper's construction—would not have been read. The play between the original module of columns, which can be easily seen from inside the nave, is also misaligned with the fifteenth-century wrapper, which suggests a more complex reading of the two grids.

In Rimini, in order to make the fifteenth-century additions work but avoid making a fifteenth-century church, Alberti proposed a purposeful contrast with the classically inspired wrapper. As a result, the church is now made up of two sets of dialectical pairs. One pair is the original condition that exists as A, plus a newer condition of A′. The second pair sees the original condition as a ground and the new project as a figure, as in any figure-ground context. In this case, Alberti set up the new addition of Gothic context as already preexisting. What is actually newest becomes the original, confounding temporal hierarchy. Due to the physical disjunction of the two styles, there is no physical part-to-whole relation in the church; instead, the rhythm of the bays is disjuncted from the new Gothic bays. fig. 1.47

Of Alberti's five buildings, Tempio Malatestiano is the best example of a disjunction between part and whole. Here, in the shell of an earlier Gothic church, Alberti's classical wall is a figure whose module creates a purposeful dissonance with the Gothic columnar nave. The result is a conceptually incomplete whole made up of two discordant parts, which, when added to the incomplete original, produces only a dialectical synthesis of fragments. Here we can speculate that the harmony proposed by Alberti's *concinnitas* leads to an entirely other world, where the supposed ideality of the antique becomes a fiction. Alberti's addition produces a layered reading from the central axis of the Gothic nave outward to encounter on either side a remnant of the nave, an interstitial space, and, last, a new enclosing facade. fig. 1.48
In the interstitial space there is no attempt at resolution between the Gothic reconstruction and the new classical enclosing wall facade, which is purposely left unresolved.

What is unique is the discourse between ideal and real, between Roman classical and Gothic, played out in the side facades and side chapels of the Tempio. The particular misalignment with the existing facade grid produces an unstable section. There seems to be little attempt to align the existing pillars and arches across

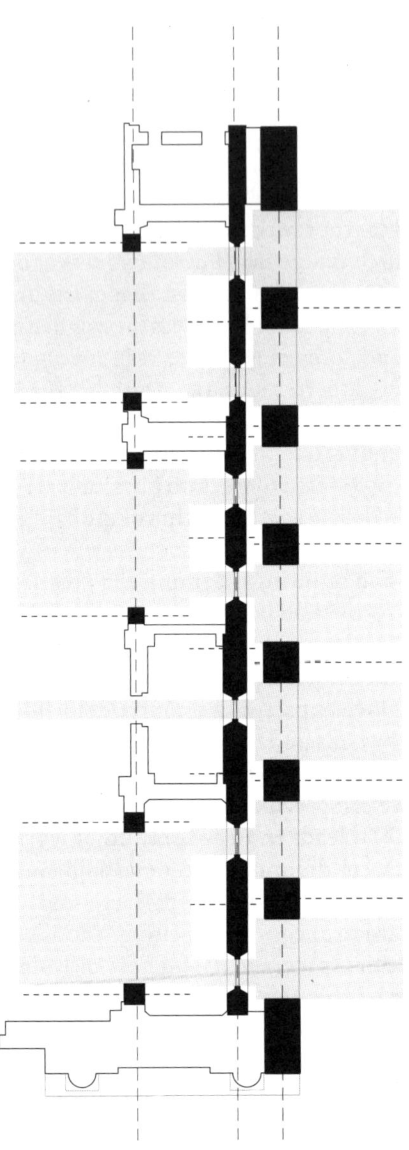

1.47 Disjunction of two styles resulting in no part-to-whole relationship, Tempio Malatestiano.

the main nave with the bay structure of Alberti's new enclosing wall. In fact, they seem to be consciously misaligned in Alberti's reconstruction, which leads to warped spatial layers in section across the central axis. What has become more interesting, in the actual space produced in the filigreed solid/void result, is this misalignment, which has been little attended to in the history of writing on Alberti. Harmony, or *concinnitas*, would have been present had Alberti aligned the new wrapper with the Gothic bay dimensions on the side facades or if both elements had been of the same style. Instead, they appear to be both consciously misaligned and stylistically different.

figs. 1.49–51

figs. 1.52–54

Conclusion

The enduring interest in Alberti is complex. The Renaissance presented a more radical change for architecture than for any other discourse. In literature, the subject matter was still literature and in painting it was still painting. But the subject matter of architecture had become different. The forms were still the same but the functions had changed, meaning the forms were no longer in a one-to-one relationship with the content. In ancient Rome, a basilica was a basilica and a triumphal arch was a triumphal arch; they were not imagined as parts of a church facade, for example. The antique and the classical styles associated with the Renaissance were a way of using building elements more as signs of their content than their specific use. Alberti's *lineamenta*, *spatium*, and *concinnitas*, and specifically the latter term, were attempts to relate the evolving social and political context to form, especially in the idea of part to whole. Alberti is important because there are two aspects of his work to consider: writing and building. While the writing was and still is a one-to-one relationship to form, the content of the buildings took on a different relationship, becoming the first conscious sign system in architecture; a sign system that proposed a two-tier relationship between form and content. Clearly Alberti recognized there was something different, even radically different, about the form/content relationship in architecture, something that had always existed but never been theorized.

Alberti unwittingly promoted the idea of part to whole, or harmony, with respect to technology (structure) and function,

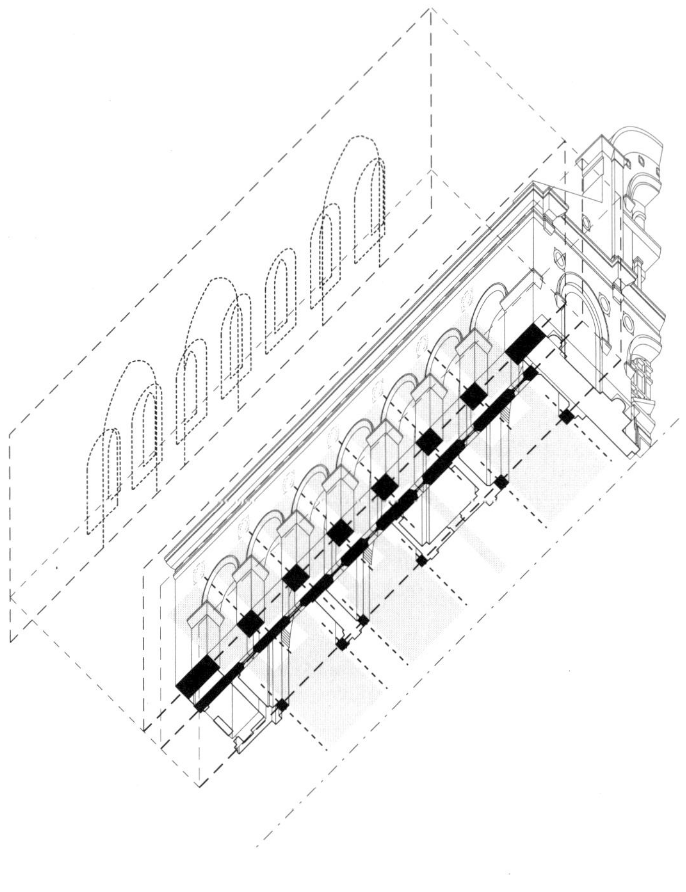

1.48 Layered reading from the central axis to Alberti's antique-inspired facade, Tempio Malatestiano.

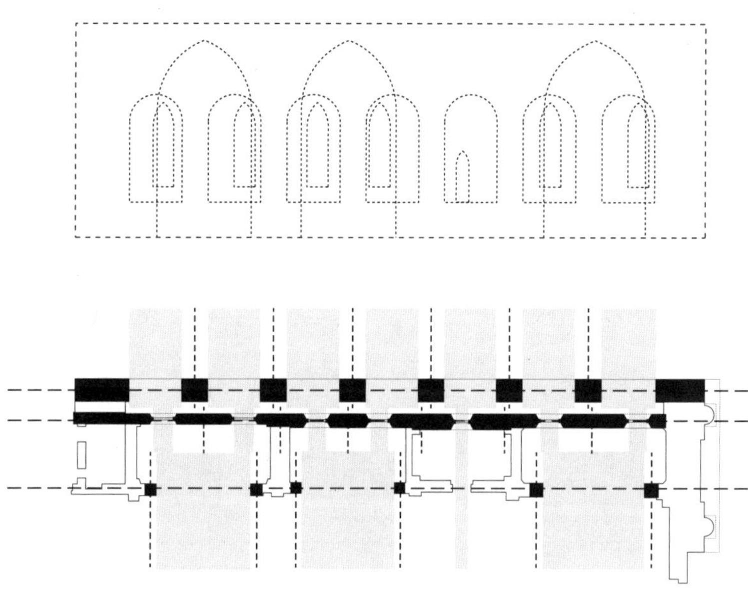

1.49 Complex "filigree" of misalignments, Tempio Malatestiano.

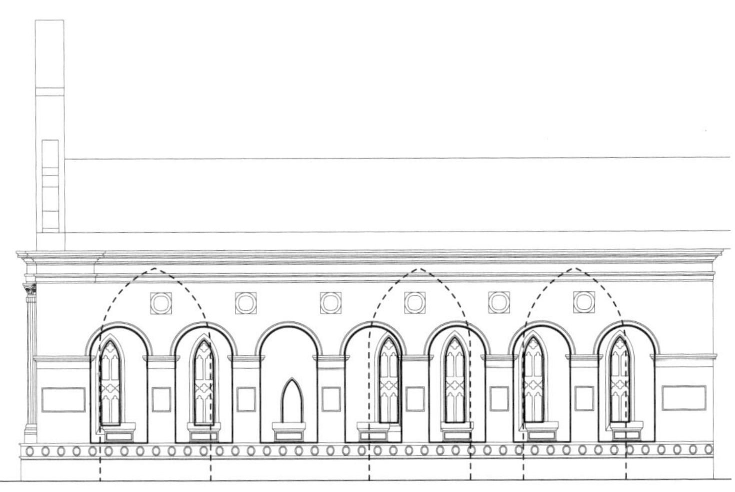

1.50 "Filigree" from exterior elevation, Tempio Malatestiano.

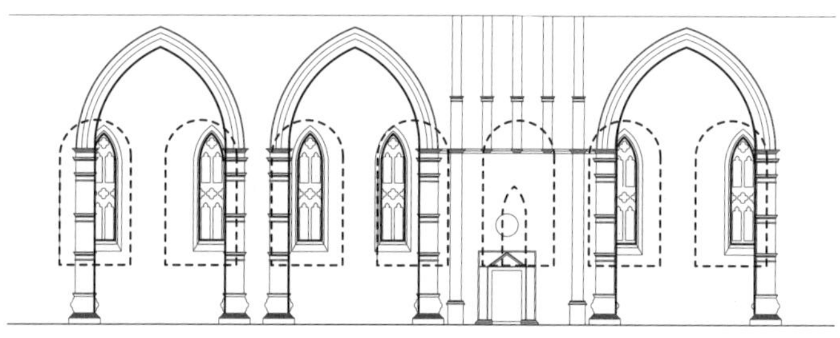

1.51 "Filigree" from interior elevation, Tempio Malatestiano.

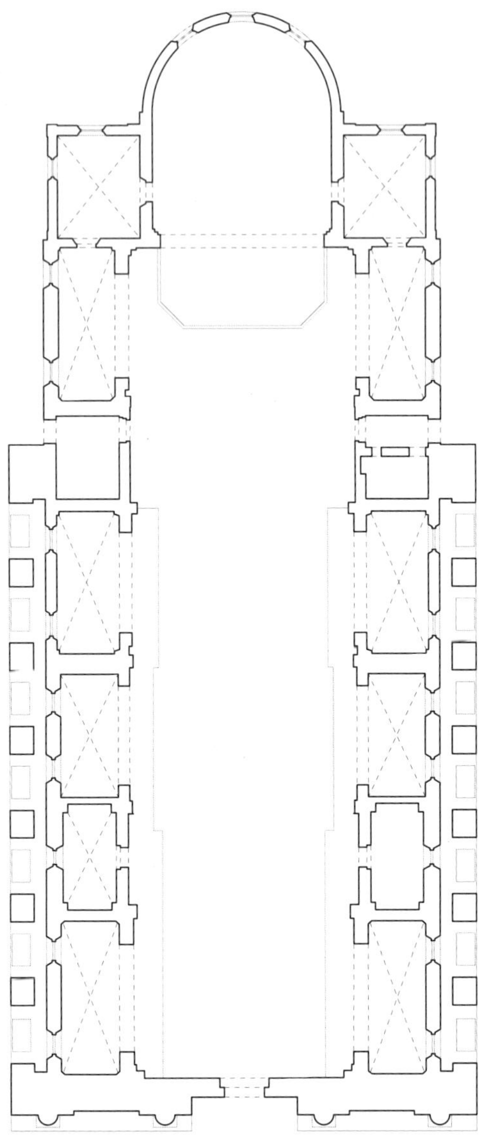

1.52 Plan, Tempio Malatestiano.

two things that other disciplines like painting and literature did not have to contend with. To counter the possibility of imitation, architecture has always brought two conditions together: precedence, which contains both style and imitation, and invention, a condition of between, of undecidability. Today, architecture can again look to philosophy, in particular to ideas in deconstruction as articulated by Jacques Derrida, for proposals that specifically counter the possibility of ideality. These include the idea of the fragment and the no longer one-to-one relationship between a sign and a thing—that is, of a free play of signifiers.

There has been little notice of how important the articulation of theory was for the absorption of modern architecture between 1914 and 1933, particularly in Europe. This is even more noticeable today, when the absence of a similar form of theoretical exploration or recollection has thrown the years of European modernism into stark relief with contemporary architecture. Now, after almost twenty-five years of little theoretical speculation, it has come to be realized that what in fact delineated the energy and ideology of the modern was the dialectic opened by theoretical speculation in direct opposition to the building project itself. Contrast this with the period of corporate modernism immediately after World War II, or even the postmodern work of James Stirling, Aldo Rossi, and Robert Venturi, each of whom had a theoretical underpinning. But there was no intrinsic dialectic that provided the synergy between writing and building. In hindsight, we can now see how writing opens up broad new vistas of thought and exploration that no "new" architecture—no building—could ever have elaborated. When Le Corbusier laid out what a revolutionary architecture should look like with his five points, he also opened up new critical possibilities for looking at all architecture. Today, the idea of the fragment might tempt us to look again at modernist theory to suggest new theoretical propositions that have little to do with the potential reappearance of modernist ideology. If this kind of theoretical opening can be said to be an aspect of any theory, then it is possible for us to look at any historical period with the idea of opening vistas previously occluded from animated recollection. It is just such a potential provocation, in the case of Leon Battista Alberti, that has led to opening up an entirely new theoretical construct found hidden in an initial postulation.

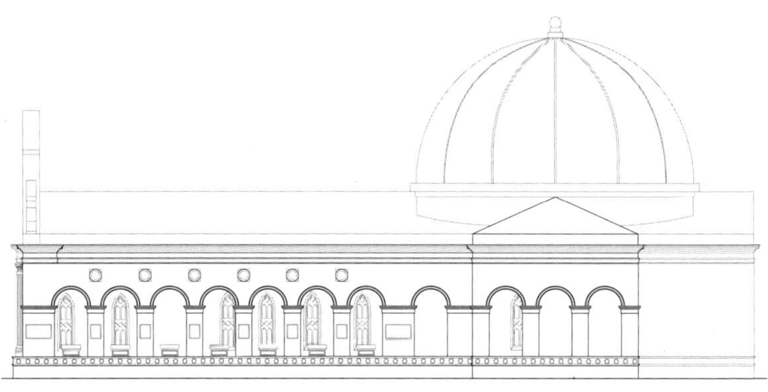

1.53 Side elevation as intended in original design, Tempio Malatestiano.

1.54 Side elevation as built, which constitutes only a fragment of Alberti's intended design, Tempio Malatestiano.

2 Alberti, Identical Copies, and the Early Modern Invention of Architectural Design

Mario Carpo

Throughout his multifarious career and his many and diverse endeavors, Leon Battista Alberti relentlessly tried to reproduce identical copies (or proportionally identical, scaled copies) of natural and cultural objects of all sorts and kinds: starting with his own texts and drawings, and including images, objects in three dimensions, existing buildings in remote and inaccessible places (such as Jerusalem), imagined buildings, human bodies and human faces in general—his own portrait in particular—and so on. One feels at times that Alberti aimed for an identical replication of nature itself, almost in its entirety—certainly a goal beyond the grasp of even the most ambitious humanist polymath.

fig. 2.1

But Alberti's almost metaphysical quest for identical copies also expressed another, more realistic preoccupation, and one that was very much in the spirit of his time. Like many of his humanist friends, Alberti worried that his writings could be tampered with, edited, altered, or otherwise transmogrified by incompetent, heedless, or foolish copyists or scribes, who—as everyone knew at the time—would frequently make changes to the texts they copied, either by accident or by design. Indeed, Alberti's new and modern notion of a unique and individual authorial identity was incompatible with the traditional technologies and cultural practices of scribal transmission. When the recording and transmission of his own writing were at stake, Alberti thought that each copy should carry and convey all and only the signs he had written. But modern print technology, which would soon provide cheap and reliable identical copies, was not yet known during most of Alberti's lifetime—and it is certainly not a coincidence that print with movable type was being developed exactly at that time, albeit unbeknownst to Alberti until his very last years. As a consequence, Alberti had to invent plenty of tricks and tools and strategies (and some were very odd indeed) in order to circumvent, or somehow limit, the risks of "unauthorized" variations inherent in all manual reproduction of texts and images. Some of his ploys are now well known: from his precocious invention of digital images for the encryption of a map of Rome, in *Descriptio urbis Romae*, and from his equally whimsical technology for the digital scan of the human body, in *De statua*, to the extraordinary, and almost quixotic, ekphrastic undertaking of his treatise on building, *De re aedificatoria*, where all architecture is discussed and described *verbis*

2.1 Leon Battista Alberti, *Self-Portrait*, circa 1435. Bronze, $7\frac{15}{16}$ by $5\frac{5}{16}$ inches. Samuel H. Kress Collection, National Gallery of Art.

solis, through words alone, and without any recourse to images or illustrations—which would have been irremediably deformed by illustrators and illuminators.[1] Alberti also used to flag passages that had to be copied with particular care, and his warnings and instructions to scribes, still readable in some extant manuscripts and even in some editions in print, have been the object of a recent study by Hartmut Wulfram.[2]

Both Alberti's pursuit of identical reproductions and his new notion of intellectual authorship (which anticipated the modern definition of copyright) would go on to have capital consequences for the history of architecture. This is proven by the many passages of *De re aedificatoria* where Alberti parses and defines, in his traditional Scholastic way, his new and revolutionary idea of authorship in building. For in Alberti's theory, drawings and physical models have a double function: the more general one of recording and transmitting visual data in space and time, and a more technical one of recording and transmitting the architect's idea of a building to the workers who will convert that idea into an actual building—which, in Alberti's theory, should be exactly the same as originally conceived by the author and expressed in his drawings and models. Today, following Nelson Goodman, such technical drawings would be called *notations*.[3]

Lineamenta, Notations, and the Homogeneity of Space

Alberti's new notational approach to architecture is set forth at the very beginning of the first book of *De re aedificatoria*, where he introduces his famous distinction between *structura*, a term that evidently refers to something built, and *lineamenta*, a term that Alberti more or less made up and no Latin dictionary will help us translate, but which manifestly appears to refer to something that is not built but imagined or drawn (with lines). None of Alberti's recent translators render *lineamenta* as "drawn project," or simply "design," in the modern sense of the term, no doubt to avoid anachronism. The elegant 1988 English translation, which is the most widely used today in the English-speaking world, translates *lineamenta* as "lineaments," which is no more eloquent in English than the original was in Latin.[4] Indeed, to understand what Alberti had in mind and what he meant by that term, one must read his treatise to the end.

As defined in Book 1, architectural lineaments are a "precise and correct outline, conceived in the mind, made up of lines and angles, and perfected in the learned intellect and imagination." At the beginning of Book 2, Alberti adds that architects must work with drawings as well as three-dimensional models throughout the conception and development of their idea (or design, in today's parlance) of a building. It is by dint of such two- and three-dimensional representations, Alberti continues, that the "author"[5] can try out his idea of a building, test it, and revise it, taking the time to invite experts, consulting them and heeding their advice. This phase of revisions, which is fundamental in Alberti's theory and which Alberti insists must be collaborative, can continue ad libitum but not ad infinitum, because the time comes when the design must be seen as completed and perfected, and thenceforth each change will only be for the worse.[6] This veritable point of no return represents a crucial watershed in Alberti's theory of building, as it marks the end of design and the beginning of construction. After this point, no redesign, doubts, or second thoughts are allowed, and construction must proceed speedily and without hesitations. For that reason, the architect's final design must include all the information that will ever be necessary to bring the building to completion. For in Alberti's theory, designers are not allowed to build, and builders are not allowed to design. Constantly fluid during the phase of invention, testing, revision, and fine-tuning, the architect's idea (and its design) thus suddenly changes state when it freezes and becomes a binding construction document, which workers must blindly obey and fully implement to the last detail. As Alberti emphasizes and reiterates, no design change should be envisaged after this line has been crossed and building on site has started.[7]

The architect's technical drawings, which the workers must be able to translate into a finished building without any additional instruction, verbal or otherwise, are thus the practical and theoretical kcystone of Alberti's new way of "building by remote control," i.e., by design and by notation. Alberti must have been aware that his new way of building required a new kind of technical drawing, which did not exist at the time and for which even the precedents of Vitruvius would have offered little help.[8] As Alberti explains in a very carefully worded passage at the beginning of the second book of *De re aedificatoria*, architects need a very special kind of drawn notations: unlike the painter's drawings, which show things as they appear to the eye, the architect's drawings must show things as they are, i.e., with real angles and lines (without foreshortening), with all measurements true to reality and proportionally drawn to scale in plan (*descriptio fundamenti*), elevation (*frons*), and side view (*latus*: unlike Raphael a few years later, Alberti never mentions sections).[9]

This crucial passage is not clearly rendered in any of the recent translations of Alberti's treatise, yet its intent is crystal clear, and when read and interpreted verbatim, it constitutes a major breakthrough in the history of architectural representations as well as the history of geometric drawings in general. For Alberti seems to envisage something here that is very close to what today we would call parallel or orthogonal or orthographic projections, which however did not and could not exist in Alberti's time.

Modern parallel projections, as defined by Gaspard Monge's descriptive geometry (1799), posit a center of projection located at infinity (the only possible point of origin for a bundle of rays or beams that are "projected" from some center and remain parallel to each other at all times). In today's projective geometry, central and parallel projections differ only in that the projection center is a proper point for the former, and an improper point (i.e., a point at infinity) for the latter. In practice, the drawing of orthogonal ground plans may not require projections of any kind, as the ground plan of a building may simply be construed as its physical imprint or trace on a real site (if necessary, redrawn to scale). But orthogonal front views, or elevations, are a trickier matter.

According to late medieval optics, and to Alberti's own theory of what today we would call central projection, as defined in his treatise *On Painting* (*De pictura*, 1435), orthogonal front views would have required an observer's eye to be physically pushed back to an infinite distance, which, as a Renaissance mathematician famously remarked, is actually "nowhere."[10] Late medieval and early modern geometries, owing to their Aristotelian framework, did not allow for such insouciant appropriations of infinity. Nor would this have been the only impediment. In Alberti's *On Painting*, a bundle of visual rays traveling from the eye to a physical object (or the other way around) at some point intersects a picture plane and leaves a trace. But if the center of projection is located very far away (and, to the limit, at infinity), this geometrical configuration would presuppose an equally infinite neutral medium through which such visual rays could travel unimpeded. As Branko Mitrovic has shown, classical notions of spatial homogeneity were not unknown in the fifteenth century: in 1417, Poggio Bracciolini's rediscovery of Lucretius's *De rerum natura* had created quite a stir among Florentine scholars.[11] Yet, for whatever reason, Alberti avoided (and in at least once instance pointedly mitigated)[12] any reference to infinite distances in space.

Today, it is easy to assume that the geometrical representation of a three-dimensional object through a set of planar drawings in plan, elevation, and side view is a banal cognitive operation, which the human mind could always figure out and perform by some kind of "tacit knowledge," prior to and without any need for geometrical definitions or explanations. Likewise, some intuitive notion of an infinite and homogeneous physical space may today appear innate to the human mind. This may be so, and many premodern, "intuitive" drawings that look like modern orthographic elevations and even sections could corroborate this argument. One generation after Alberti, Piero della Francesca drew at least one famous head in two plans, an elevation, and a side view, which are all connected by parallel projection lines.[13] fig. 2.2

Additionally, late medieval and Renaissance architects frequently used, and depended on, simpler sets of orthogonal or almost orthogonal plans, elevations, and side views (and later, sections). But no mathematician at the time could have defined, let alone formalized, any such figures as projections, for lack of a workable notion of geometric infinity. The homogeneous and infinite space of modern science may appear intuitive to modern scientists, but it was seldom intuited (and, more crucially, none of these intuitions ever went mainstream) before the rise of modern science. As Alberti could famously provide a modern definition of central projections in his treatise *On Painting*, one could surmise that a mathematical definition of parallel projections should have been almost within the reach of late medieval science. Instead, parallel projections were, for more than three centuries, a practice without a theory.[14]

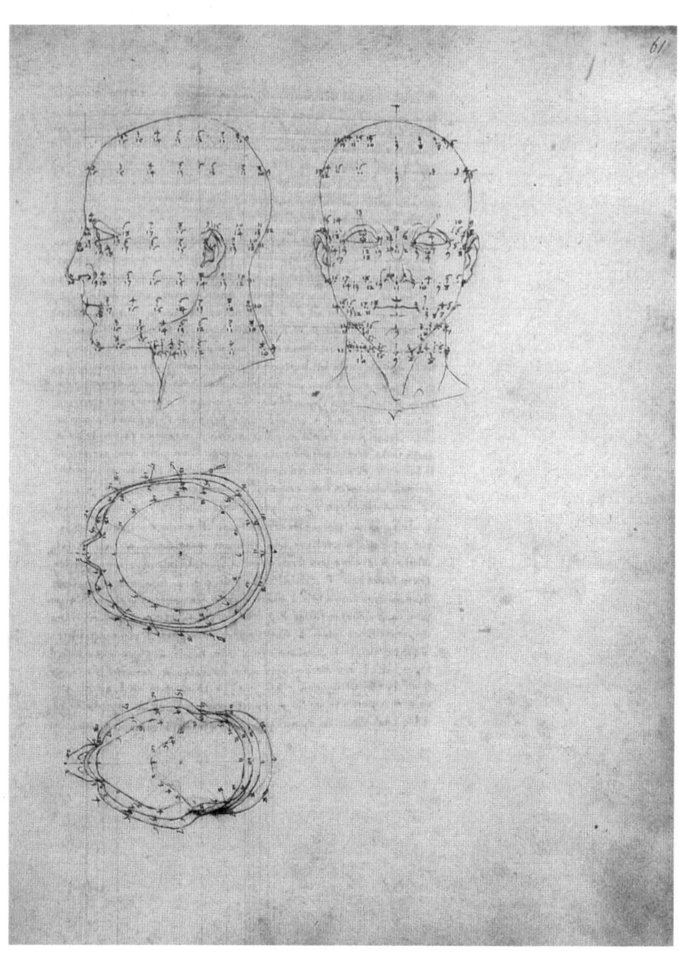

2.2 Piero della Francesca, projection of a human head, from *De prospectiva pingendi* (On the perspective of painting), 1474–1482, Biblioteca Palatina, Parma.

Yet in this matter, too, Alberti scored a major breakthrough. Precisely because he had already defined central projections in his treatise on painting, when a few years later he wrote his treatise on architecture Alberti could, for the first time ever, lay out precisely what architects should *not* do: architects should avoid perspective, as from foreshortened lines one cannot take precise measurements (in Raphael's later wording).[15] One needs perspective to have been invented in order to tell architects not to use it. As a side effect of his invention of geometrical perspective, Alberti could provide the first (albeit negative) geometrical definition of modern proportional and orthogonal plans and elevations—at a time when geometry did not allow for any definition of parallel projections. This may appear to be a fine point, of geometry (and it is, as it is tantamount to defining parallel projections as "noncentral" projections, without a corresponding center of projection at infinity); but at a more practical level, Alberti's strategy was also consistent with the basic need to explain why scaled elevation drawings should not include foreshortened lines (as such drawings often did before Alberti, and occasionally kept doing well after him). Alberti's aim was to define a new kind of technical notation that would allow a designer to fully, univocally, and unambiguously determine all aspects of a three-dimensional building using a set of planar drawings. As this ambition was evidently beyond the reach of the geometry of his time, it is not surprising that Alberti ended up inventing something similar to modern parallel projections, hence positing the need for the mathematical definition of a homogeneous space where such projections could occur—some three hundred and fifty years before Monge wrote down the rules we still study at school.[16]

Allography, Authorship, and Intellectual Ownership

Alberti reiterates and emphasizes this notion of a point of no return separating the intellectual invention of a building from its material execution at the end of Book 9, almost at the close of his treatise, immediately following one of the most important theoretical parts of it, on the definition of proportional beauty. "Facere . . . non magis architecti est quam operarii fabri":[17]

making is for manual workers, and none of the architect's business. For that reason, architects would be well advised not to dabble in the practicalities of the building site—indeed, perhaps they should not even set foot on it. Likewise, Alberti holds that an architect should not intervene as a clerk of the works, site manager, or supervisor; those roles are best left to others. In short, architects should limit themselves to providing clients with sound advice and clean drawings ("fidum consilium . . . castigataque lineamenta").[18]

It may not always be easy, Alberti concedes, to oblige someone else to execute something exactly as one has conceived it; nonetheless, the intentions of all "authors" must be respected, regardless of all practical impediments, even after their death.[19] The term Alberti uses here, *auctor*, is even more meaningful and revealing, as in Alberti's treatise the term occurs both in its etymological sense (from *augeo/-ere*, the one who makes something grow or increase, hence the instigator, protector, or creator of something), and in its classical meaning of "source," or "model" (as in the expression "veteres auctores"). The new authorial status that Alberti bestows on architects, now seen as intellectual inventors and not as artisanal makers, is the most influential and lasting legacy of his architectural theory, and the keystone of what I have elsewhere called the "Albertian paradigm" in architecture. In Alberti's theory, architects are both "creators" and "authors," in the modern sense of the term—the inventors of objects they do not really make, but which are nevertheless seen as objects of their making, and which they own in part, in some abstract way, even if the objects legally belong to someone else who paid for them and can use them and sell them. Today this form of abstract ownership, which Alberti was only envisaging, pertains to the domain of intellectual property rights—a foundation of the modern industrial world that did not exist before the rise of industrial modernity (and, not coincidentally, one that is already disappearing from the social and legal practices of digital postmodernity).

The idea that architecture may entail some form of intellectual ownership, and that the inventor or designer of a building may maintain some form of abstract, ideal ownership of a building that is built for and materially owned by others, is today more or less taken for granted, but in Alberti's time this notion, then so novel and revolutionary, must have sounded utterly outlandish; for most of Alberti's contemporaries it probably made no sense at all. Alberti was certainly aware of, and he was probably taking stock of and reacting to, one monumental precedent. Only one generation before him, going counter to the guild-based, collaborative way of building that was common at the end of the Middle Ages, Brunelleschi had striven to be seen as the sole inventor of a major building—the dome of the cathedral of Florence; but to do so he had come up with a quite different solution.

Throughout the eighteen years it took to build the dome, Brunelleschi never left the site—except to enact some famous stratagems that were meant to prove that without him the guilds and workers would have been at their wits' end, and would not have known what to do. For eighteen years, day in and day out, Brunelleschi distilled instructions only on site, viva voce, as and when needed—as Antonio Manetti recounts, it was as if he had laid each brick in person.[20] Brunelleschi never put his project or design on paper—or at least not in a way that would have allowed others to keep building without him. To the last day, the overall idea of the building stayed with him, a secret to all.[21] When the building was finished and inaugurated—and, indeed, unanimously recognized as the fruit of his ingenuity—Brunelleschi, as the craftsman he was, could have claimed, "This building is mine because from start to finish I made it all with my own hands, or almost," implying that all other hands on site, and he evidently needed many, were just carrying out his orders.

Alberti's solution to the then nascent problem of architectural authorship was quite different, far more economic and functional, and, as we now know, it would be the winner in the long run. Working in the Albertian way, the new, modern "authorial" architect could now claim, "This building is mine not because I made it with my hands, but because I conceived it and made a drawing of it; my drawing has been seen and discussed by many, then approved by my patrons, and everyone can see that the building as built is identical to the one I had originally invented and drawn"—or as we would say today, designed. This transition from building to drawing signals the transition from the autographic identity of a traditional maker (someone who crafts an object in person and with his own hands) to the allographic status of most modern design—where objects are conceived by someone but realized by others, exclusively on the basis of the author's instructions or notations.[22] The same shift also marks the historical transition from medieval "arts" as mechanical crafts to modern "fine arts," also known as the "arts of drawing," which were indeed invented in the Renaissance, and architecture was one of them.

The Rise and Fall of the Notational Paradigm

Notations are the keystone of the Albertian way of building by design. When working in the Albertian, notational way, the separation in principle between design and construction would require architects to use a notational system that is precise and robust enough to predetermine a building in its entirety—a rather problematic epistemological and ontological requirement. In the case of architecture, objects are mostly three-dimensional, whereas the notations used to describe them tend to be planar; moreover, most architectural drawings and models must be, for practical reasons, much smaller than the objects they represent. Indeed, all geometry, from the beginning of times to modern post-Euclidian science, can be seen as a data compression technology used to notate big three-dimensional objects on small, flat sheets of paper. Everyone can see the advantage of having every aspect and feature of a big building inscribed in a single batch or roll of blueprints; but in order to work that way, all notational languages are bound to simplify and cut corners; and, as we know, no language is universal, and none neutral. Consequently, the inevitable corollary of the Albertian notational paradigm in architecture is that modern architects can only build what they can notate—i.e., what they can make a usable, measurable geometric drawing of: a drawing that will convey to builders enough geometrical data for that object to be built as intended. This notational bottleneck is a historical variable, as it depends on the complexity of the geometric shapes architects have in mind, and the potency of the geometric tools they have at their disposal to notate them. This is one reason why potato-like shapes have seldom been built in the history of modern architecture: potatoes (now known as blobs) are easy to make—any sculptor with a block of clay can make one—but difficult to notate geometrically, because there is no geometric or generative rule embedded in them, and the position of each point in space must be independently measured and recorded in three dimensions (*x*, *y*, and *z*). Depending on the number of points to be measured this way, this can be a very toilsome labor if performed by hand. And this is of course where, starting from the early 1990s, computers have been a game changer: given their almost infinite processing power, they can notate blobs almost as easily as boxes—and at the same cost, or almost.[23]

Today, long after the digital turn started to upend many principles and practices of architectural design, it is not clear to what extent this drastic surge in our power to store and process geometrical notations should be seen as an extension, or a reversal, of the Albertian notational paradigm. From the beginning, designers used computers to scan and notate free forms (i.e., objects, like potatoes, that do not follow any geometrical rule) as well as to generate advanced geometrical objects (i.e., forms determined by complex mathematical functions like splines, topological surfaces, etc.). Both approaches have vastly expanded the repertoire of forms that architects can design and build, but neither disproves the notational principles inherent in the Albertian way of building. Things are likely to be changing again now, as a new approach to computation, based on "big data" and artificial intelligence, is prompting a drastic reset of our entire scientific framework. This may be the real demise of the Albertian paradigm in architecture, which in turn should come as no surprise if the big data revolution turns out to be, as many believe, the most drastic shift in the history of Western science since its Greek beginnings—or at least since the rise of the modern, analytic and predictive experimental method.[24]

By contrast, the modernity of the Albertian ideological project is even more striking if seen in the cultural and technological context in which Alberti first formulated it. In Alberti's theory, the architect's design is an almost mechanical matrix that is expressed, or rather imprinted, metaphorically speaking, in a physical object when this is materialized and built in three dimensions. This translation from drawing to building is a purely mechanical operation, devoid of any intellectual added value, and as such it falls outside the scope of the architect's action, both in theory and in practice.

Evidently, this new way of building by notation would have been impossible to implement at the time of Alberti's writing, for cultural as well as for practical reasons. Alberti himself found that out to his detriment when, relatively late in life, he started a new career as an architect and tried to put his theory into practice. Sent from Rome to Rimini on November 18, 1454, his letter to Matteo de' Pasti, the local sculptor and medalist who served as a middleman between the absentee designer and the builders of Alberti's uncompleted church of San Francesco, or Tempio Malatestiano, in

fig. 2.3 Rimini, is an almost pathetic testimony of Alberti's frustration.[25]

The letter proves that Alberti had indeed provided exhaustive construction drawings and at least one model for the building, but that the workers on site built as they saw fit. Alberti found out and wrote to complain, reiterating the reasons for his design choices and explaining how every part of his design was justified and necessary, referring the workers once again to his drawings and models, and concluding, somewhat peevishly, that his design was so carefully thought out that with the slightest change "all its music breaks down [si discorda tutta quella musica]." It is not known whether the workers could not understand Alberti's drawings, whether they thought—rightly—that they were under no obligation to abide by them, or both.

In this instance, once again, Alberti's theory proved to be ahead of the technical means and social practices of his time. It is nevertheless to him that we owe the tenet, crucial for modernity, of a clear-cut separation between intellectual conception and material execution, hence the modern distinction and separation between the architect as a maker of drawings and the artisan worker as a maker of objects. Likewise, Alberti's theoretical revolution invented the modern architect as a humanist author, the modern definition of architecture as an allographic art, and the modern definition of architectural design as a technology of notation, with all the social, technical, formal, and aesthetic consequences that implies. Alberti did not invent architecture, but he invented the architect, as well as the architectural profession as we know it (or rather knew it, till the digital turn started to change some rules of the game). And the origin of all that was a principle, simple and strong: the drawing is the architect's real creation; the building is only its copy—but as always, in Alberti's theory, an identical copy.

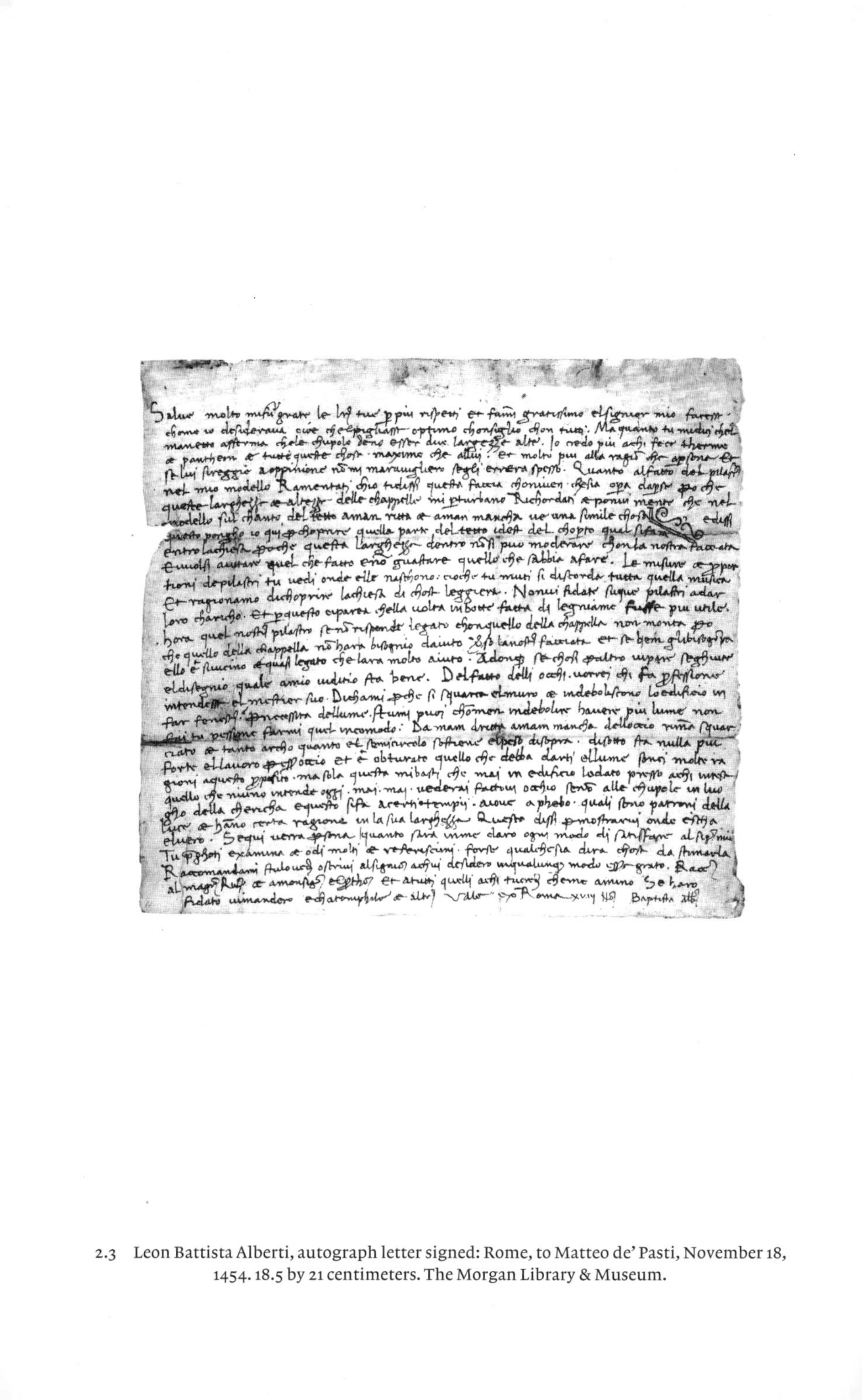

2.3 Leon Battista Alberti, autograph letter signed: Rome, to Matteo de' Pasti, November 18, 1454. 18.5 by 21 centimeters. The Morgan Library & Museum.

From Notational Art to Notational Work

The medieval builder was an artisan who toiled on site, come rain or shine. The Albertian architect is an intellectual laborer who conceives and composes clean drawings from the quiet of an office and offers professional advice for a fee.[26] A few centuries later, designers who still earn their living that way have reasons to be grateful to Alberti, for without him they would still be carving wood, laying bricks, and cutting stones—making buildings, instead of making drawings. But what about those on the receiving end of the Albertian revolution? If architecture becomes a notational art (art that is scripted by some but executed by others), building must become notational work: work that is executed by some, but scripted by others.

The socioeconomic implications of Alberti's new subdivision of labor are no less momentous than the artistic ones. Construction workers, who in the medieval guild system were skilled, independent artisans working together as associates in something similar to a modern cooperative, become hired hands: centuries before the industrial revolution, proletarians by deeds, if not yet by name. Wage labor was not forbidden in corporate city-states, but in Alberti's ideological project all work is by definition hired work, because his deskilled workers are reduced to labor force—not in the Marxist but in the mechanical sense of the term: animal energy, as we would say today, needed to execute the plans laid out by the Albertian designer.

Alberti never doubted that construction workers would be capable and happy to work that way. The Rimini incident proved otherwise. And apparently, Alberti never suspected that some building materials may at times be quirky or unwieldy, thus requiring some degree of inventiveness, intelligence, and impromptu problem-solving on site. Design adjustments were Alberti's bête noire; his was a Laplacian, clockwork universe of absolute human and material predictability—two centuries before the rise of modern science.[27] With hindsight, today we also know that while Alberti's notational mandate was ostensibly meant for, and limited to, architecture and construction work, his new way of making had the potential to be applied to the way we make almost everything. And that's exactly what happened over time: the Albertian authorial paradigm, where ideation is separated from material realization, became a sociotechnical staple of industrial modernity. In the Albertian system, as in the modern world in general, thinkers don't make, and makers don't think; the Albertian worker doesn't really work: he executes a script.

Early in the twentieth century, Alberti's notational mode of production was powerfully reinstated by Frederick Winslow Taylor's *Principles of Scientific Management* (1911), one of the theoretical foundations of the modern industrial system. Taylor, a Philadelphia Quaker, was a mechanical engineer by training, and nothing in his life, career, and published work suggests that he ever even heard the name of Leon Battista Alberti. Yet, more than four centuries apart, Alberti and Taylor faced a curiously similar problem. Alberti had to deskill a vast population of highly proficient, trained artisans to make space for his newfangled "authorial" designer; Taylor had to cope with a vast population of unskilled, mostly immigrant manual laborers and find a way to exploit their physical force without training them. He did not have to "deskill" them because they had no skills to begin with, and Taylor's system was designed to keep them that way. As Taylor's manual workers were supposedly incapable of making even the most elementary rational decisions, each of their gestures at work had to be fully scripted by others: in Taylor's scientific management, the agency of each worker is limited to executing instructions.[28]

Twentieth-century Taylorism brought Alberti's notational project to industrial shop work, then to the factory floor, and ultimately to the culture, economy, and society of the machine-made environment. Based on today's generally accepted chronology of European history, Alberti was a medieval man, born and bred in the Middle Ages. He was also famously a polymath—a universal man. Not surprisingly, his multifarious work reveals many, often widely contradictory facets, which have been variously interpreted over time. Yet, for historians of architecture and for historians of technology alike, a bigger picture now emerges, suggesting that Alberti's humanism may have been one of the most cogent and pertinent harbingers of modern art, science, technology, and even of industrial modernity at large.

3 Tafuri on Alberti: Architecture's "Desperate Solitude" and the Crisis of Humanist Representation

Daniel Sherer

When the past speaks it always speaks as an oracle: only if you are an architect of the future and know the present will you understand it.

—Friedrich Nietzsche, *On the Advantages and Disadvantages of History for Life* (1874)

Manfredo Tafuri transformed our understanding of Alberti in a number of areas.[1] One stands out in particular: the close relationship Alberti established in his architectural theory and practice with a concept of representation aware of its own limits and detached from the metaphysical certainties often associated with his thought. Reframing the problem in this way allowed Tafuri to question and ultimately to overturn reigning assumptions about Alberti, the most prominent of which maintained that harmonic analogism, as this concept was understood by Rudolf Wittkower in his seminal *Architectural Principles in the Age of Humanism* (1949), was a defining feature both of humanist principles in general and of Alberti's theorization of them.[2]

By challenging the primacy of these "principles," Tafuri upended the system of normative categories that had shaped the image of Alberti for over half a century. The historian who, more than any other, defined this image was Wittkower himself, who elaborated a reassuring postwar reading of Alberti that inscribed the work of the humanist architect within the main line of Western classicism (even if the chapter on Alberti was written, in fact, during the war).[3] For him, it was essential to remind a generation shaken by global conflict that one of the most famous architects of the age of humanism upheld a universalizing idea of harmony. When Tafuri broke with this normative reading, Alberti suddenly reappeared in an unexpected guise, not as the serene proponent of Neoplatonic analogism but as the subversive theoretician of an architecture whose disciplinary foundations were unstable. Alberti's humanist project ceased to be understood as a straightforward, if highly selective, recuperation of the antique lexicon. Instead this project, and the architecture of the Renaissance it helped inaugurate, became a theater of tensions in which nothing remains of the radiant harmony of the classical legacy save for an oblique and refracted memory.[4]

Once Alberti is seen from this standpoint, two related shifts occur: first, widely accepted commonplaces regarding the harmonic coherence of his architecture are shown to be untenable; second, Alberti's impact on the subsequent development of the classical language reveals unsuspected areas of reception. Characterized in equal measure by rupture and continuity, this reception is neither unilinear nor homogeneous. Indeed, Tafuri argued that Alberti's "difficult lesson" was often betrayed by those who saw themselves as his heirs: in this respect the "tranquillizing interpretations" to which *De re aedificatoria* lent itself "cast a veil of oblivion over the tragic, even overwhelming consciousness of the limits of *techne* and the arbitrariness of norms" inscribed within the Albertian project.[5] To test this hypothesis it will be necessary to examine works by Francesco di Giorgio and Giuliano da Sangallo in the fifteenth century and by Bramante, Raphael, Giulio Romano, and Palladio in the sixteenth. In other words, all of these architects, when pursuing divergent readings of Alberti, fell short of grasping the full complexity of his theoretical contribution. If one takes Tafuri at his word about this collective lapse (and there is no reason not to), one might surmise that it did not impede but may have actually contributed to the diversity and originality of the readings in question.

For Tafuri, Alberti was both *exemplary* and *exceptional*: as the inventor of a form of theoretical knowledge and an architectural language that resist conventional interpretations, Alberti was the author of the most comprehensive corpus of normative principles until the appearance of Palladio's *Quattro libri* (1570).[6] Here it is worth recalling two striking phrases from *Venice and the Renaissance* (1985) that capture what is essential in his interpretation of Alberti, while offering new insight into what Alberti and Palladio shared in some fundamental sense. For what both architect/theorists produced were not modes of order grounded in concepts of Neoplatonic harmony, as Wittkower maintained, but rather "finite islands of rationality" tragically isolated from their contexts, "hermetic architectural objects . . . that display their own desperate solitude."[7]

Such characterizations are integral parts of Tafuri's densely layered prose, which sharply diverges from that of other architectural historians in many respects. One can see this above all in its complex use of metaphor which, in opening up spaces of intensified meaning, reinforces the narrative at key points. What we are dealing with here is nothing less than what Hans Blumenberg has called a *metaphorology*: a sophisticated employment of rhetorical tropes that lends vividness to any given argument by revealing the range of connotation of its conceptual framework.[8] When constructing this framework, Tafuri marshals a relatively restricted number of concepts, among which *autonomy*, *heteronomy*, *ideology*, *utopia*, *rationalization*, and *crisis* are privileged instances of his theoretical vocabulary. This array of concepts, through the metaphors that are intimately associated with them, dramatizes the historical unfolding of the discipline in the work of its key protagonists, illuminating their role within wider cycles of architectural language. In this way metaphor and concept work together to further Tafuri's historiographical purposes.[9]

Nowhere is this more evident than in his reading of Alberti. In a more specific sense, this metaphorical dimension of Tafuri's historiography invites us to ponder the following questions: In what ways are Alberti's built projects set apart from their contexts, as so many "islands of rationality"? Is their isolation a function of their form, or are other factors involved? What is the nature of this rationality? Why is such "isolation" "tragic"? And if it is as Tafuri claims it to be, what sort of tragedy are we dealing with? In what follows I shall try to answer these questions by showing how Tafuri drew connections between disparate areas of Alberti's achievement, elucidating the relation of his architecture to its historical contexts in light of the multiple uses of representation that defined the humanist era.[10]

One important instrument Tafuri utilized when trying to decode these uses was polycentric analysis.[11] This method of interpretation illuminates the architectural project by tracing the multiplicity of external factors that simultaneously shape it, reinserting a given work of architecture into its various contexts in ways that radically put into question traditional notions of intellectual specialization.[12] It is decisive for such an approach that architecture not only is enmeshed in a dense web of relationships, but that it retains some measure of independence even when being so profoundly interconnected. The object of this method was the ensemble of stratified knowledges that enter into architecture no less than the worlds of, science, technology, politics and commerce that condition it.[13] By adopting this multifaceted approach, Tafuri showed that Alberti was the first to situate architecture as a humanist project that stands out from the complex reality of the city in its unremitting concentration on form and on the related concept of *finitio*, which may be translated as "coherent profile" or "measured outline."[14] According to the Italian historian, Alberti's architecture, by virtue of its formal resolution, subtly yet decisively distances itself from the very urban texture of which it is a constitutive part.

The importance of this aspect of Tafuri's reading of Alberti should not be underestimated, if only because the thesis of *isolated form*, understood to be a defining characteristic of the *all'antica* language, might well be taken to be the dark underside of the first stirrings of autonomy in our discipline: a hermeneutic possibility that refers as much to the architect as subject as to the architectural object. This dual reference is decisive for understanding Alberti's place within Tafuri's historical project. Alberti, in fact, was a frequent presence in Tafuri's historiography from 1968 onward, assuming an increasingly prominent role in the final phases of his trajectory.[15] This can be seen in Tafuri's placement of Alberti's emblem of the winged eye, which originally adorned the reverse of the medal executed by Matteo de' Pasti (1446–1450), on the cover of fig. 3.1 his last book, *Ricerca del Rinascimento: Principi, città, architetti* (Turin, 1992), the English translation of which, *Interpreting the Renaissance: Princes, Cities, Architects*, appeared in 2006.[16]

Exemplifying Alberti's fascination with allegory and oblique expression, this enigmatic symbol of the celerity of vision and the power of theoretical insight signifies the uncertainties of the sign in a world that is equally unstable. The power of visuality, matrix of representation and figure of thought, is here undercut by the irony of the laconic motto, which takes the form of an insistent question: QUID TUM?, So what?, expressing the profound disenchantment that Tafuri shared with his great humanist predecessor, as Massimo Cacciari pointed out.[17] As part of Tafuri's incisive critique of Wittkower, the choice of this ambiguous emblem for the cover of his last book accentuates the dissonance that is present even where *concinnitas* is strongest, the problem of the unfinished, so poignant in the architect who theorized the *finitio* of the built

3.1 *Quid Tum*, Flying Eye, emblem of Alberti from a medal cast by Matteo de' Pasti. Designed by Alberti, 1446–1450.

project, and, ultimately, the tragic finitude of human existence, which only the fame of the architect can overcome.[18]

Tafuri's new conception of Alberti achieved its fullest articulation in the essay "Discordant Harmony from Alberti to Zuccari" (1979), building on earlier insights elaborated in *Theories and History* (1968). Eugenio Garin's discussion of the anguished dimension of Alberti, cited at the beginning of the text, sets the tone for the entire argument: "Alberti did not paint his most striking pictures, he set them down in words, chasing the disorder of the unforeseeable particular, the futility of an existence hung between malice and good fortune, beyond the realm of reason, beyond the universal order of nature, to a place providence abandoned."[19] Pursuing an interpretive path opened by Garin, while moving toward a critical horizon that Garin could not have anticipated, Tafuri read Alberti dialectically, as an architect caught between the humanist aspiration to revive the classical language and a sharp awareness of the precariousness of this project.[20] Tafuri subjected this cultural rebirth, customarily called the Renaissance, to a reassessment that was as comprehensive as it was radical, aimed at clearing the field of antiquated commonplaces and historiographical relics. A new look at Alberti was central to this project of rewriting the significance of this cultural movement. For to rewrite Alberti is in a sense also to reevaluate what came after him and what he shaped from afar, especially in the two centuries between his birth and the death of Palladio, his greatest follower and the reinventor of the classical code that both championed, animated by an acute awareness of the exceptions that proliferate where it held sway.

When pursuing the implications of this reading, we can identify six ways in which Tafuri can be said to have transformed our view of Alberti and of the tension-filled *rinascita* which he helped inaugurate: (1) by foregrounding strategies of linguistic ambiguity implied by Alberti's confrontation of stylistic codes; (2) by reassessing the use of classical *exempla* in the new humanist stance toward history; (3) by emphasizing the importance of the dialectic of rule and invention, and hence also that of the exception to accepted norms as a way of understanding the *virtù* of the architect in its dual contest with *fortuna* and time; (4) by valorizing the role of artifice and representation in architecture conceived to be a point of contact with painting and perspective in particular;

(5) by investigating the limits of *techne* and all that it implies for the refusal of overambitious projects, underscoring Alberti's complex attitude regarding the domination of nature; and, finally, (6) by examining the different receptions of Alberti by humanist architects from the fifteenth to the late sixteenth centuries, both in terms of their irreducible specificity and in light of wider theoretical issues and patterns of cultural signification.

Santa Maria Novella: "The Contaminated Seduction of Linguistic Pluralism"

We can approach Tafuri's interpretation of Alberti by turning first to Santa Maria Novella (c. 1450) (fig. 1.5), a project that in his view is symptomatic of the contradictions that traverse Alberti's oeuvre. This is the case, above all, because the part that is Alberti's carries on an uneasy coexistence with the medieval portions of the structure, with which the new humanist code strikes up a complex and ambivalent dialogue.[21] Tafuri's reading of this dialogue in his *Theories and History of Architecture* (1968) emphasizes its conflictual nature: "Alberti ... quarrels continuously with the pre-existing structures on which he grafts his new interventions."[22] Instead of Wittkower's ideal harmonies and unity of classical form and philosophical content, we are confronted by a series of conflicts and ambiguities, some of which are explicit, others more difficult to detect.[23] Yet all, when taken together, are phenomena of considerable importance whose investigation can help revise our understanding of the humanist architectural universe that Alberti, along with Brunelleschi, is responsible for inaugurating.

Tafuri identifies the principal difference between Alberti's approach and Brunelleschi's in the following way: "But when Alberti lets the Medieval evidence seep through the facade of S. Maria Novella, his goals are not as linear and absolute as those in Brunelleschi's work. On the one hand, Alberti wants to make tangible the ideal unity of the classicist language: he therefore leaves breathing space for the pre-existing Gothic elements ... to dramatise, to represent and perpetuate the heroic victory of Humanist reason over Medieval or Medievalizing 'barbarisms.'

On the other hand he realizes this game is extremely dangerous, because he himself discovers, through it, the contaminated seduction of linguistic pluralism."[24] He then specifies the outcome of this approach as "the exasperated need to specify the classical code through historical verification," which is "the result of the insecurity reflected in so many pages of *De re aedificatoria*."[25] Tafuri concludes: "The entire culture of the sixteenth century swings between these two poles: on the one hand the will to give historical foundation to an anti-historical code, like the one of the revived Classicism, and on the other hand, the temptation, repressed but always there, to compromise and dirty one's hands with the very Medieval and Gothic languages that the entire Classicist culture wanted to erase."[26]

"Contaminated seduction of linguistic pluralism"; "exasperated need to specify the classical code"; "the temptation to compromise and dirty one's hands": when placed in the context of Tafuri's discursive strategies as they developed from *Theories and History* to "Discordant Harmony," these striking formulations—in which metaphorical expression appears to gain the upper hand over the thought expressed, even if the former is ultimately subordinated to the latter—suggest that Alberti, unlike Brunelleschi, was acutely aware that to revive the classical while respecting the medieval was to serve two masters, putting the architect in a well-nigh-impossible position.[27] The point is a fundamental one, since instead of a unitary classical origin for Alberti's architectural language, what is being proposed is more complex: a clash between competing codes. Alberti's historical specificity becomes evident in this clash, which exposes the latent ideological and cultural tensions in his theory and practice.

In his exploration of these constitutive tensions, Tafuri has little to say, in the earlier phases of his historiographical *iter*, about their specific historical circumstances. This is not entirely surprising since at this moment in his trajectory, from 1968 to 1979, Tafuri was primarily concerned with tracing architecture's internal articulations in light of the discovery and subsequent eclipse of history in architecture from the Renaissance to the twentieth century, and less with what would later be his focus, the multiple contexts that impinge on the architectural project. His attention to these forces would come into its own only in the 1980s, when he extended his historical project in new directions.[28] Between the two phases of his trajectory Tafuri drew out the implications of his pivotal concept of architectural ideology, first in "Per una critica dell'ideologia architettonica" (1969) and then in *Architecture and Utopia* (1973), which marshaled arguments that enabled him to navigate the discipline's extremes of autonomy and heteronomy.[29]

At this point Tafuri was concerned with tracing the margins of autonomy of architecture that allowed it to operate, often just barely, under capitalist conditions (at the price of near-total ideologization).[30] Simultaneously, he was investigating the historical developments that gave rise to these conditions. Each of the oppositions that these conditions presuppose (architectural project/socioeconomic circumstances; autonomy/heteronomy) is inscribed in diverse theoretical, epistemic, and historical contexts, all of which were affected, at times more profoundly, at times less, by the architectural projects Tafuri examined. Starting with the era of humanism, he concentrated on the roles played by Brunelleschi and Alberti as key proponents of the *all'antica* code, following their dual moves of *pietas* and violation and their impact into the sixteenth century, on to the contest of Borromini and Bernini in the seventeenth, culminating with the most explosive manifestation of crisis the classical language ever experienced in Piranesi. As to Tafuri's earlier conception of the internal articulations of the code, and more specifically his analysis of the ways in which disparate languages interact and compete in any given work of architecture, these do not refer in this instance to any reductive use of the formalist legacy but to something more philologically precise and hermeneutically cogent: an acute awareness of the semantic crisis that came out into the open with Alberti's practice.[31] This reading revealed what was at stake with the advent of Brunelleschi's classicizing project, while enabling a grasp of the instabilities that came to light when Alberti's *all'antica* discourse was confronted by the Gothic past, opening a space of contradiction due to the clash between diverse stylistic codes and stratified languages.

In fact, the link between the return of the (historical) repressed—in this case, the Gothic tradition—and the humanist crisis of codes is an important if often overlooked component of

Tafuri's historical analysis, acting as a red thread in his discussion of the tensions within classicism from *Theories and History* (1968) through "Discordant Harmony" (1979) to *Interpreting the Renaissance* (1992). To clarify its ramifications Tafuri combined his critique of Wittkower's idea of humanist principles with a critical reframing of Erwin Panofsky's theses on perspective—a topic to which he devoted an in-depth analysis in *Theories and History* drawing out its implications for Renaissance architectural culture.[32] And yet it is in another of Panofsky's contributions—one that Tafuri does not cite—that one finds a compelling response to the clash of languages manifest in Alberti's intervention in Santa Maria Novella. In his essay "The First Page of Giorgio Vasari's *Libro*," Panofsky outlined three options for the humanist architect confronted by the Gothic: complete reformulation of the existing parts, continuity with the earlier style, or the articulation of a middle way between the two.[33] Alberti seems to choose the third option. Yet since he does so to bring about the triumph of classicism over the Gothic, Tafuri argues that this decision is tantamount to choosing the first option. As a result, he only succeeds in digging himself deeper into an uncertain historicist operation beset by risk. Tafuri's attempt to capture the specificity of Alberti's approach in this respect is central to his understanding of the architect's ambiguous humanist undertaking. In so doing Tafuri uncovers the darker anxieties and overall sense of crisis that marks Alberti's contribution to Renaissance architecture.

The effects of the crisis are visible above all in the handling of the preexisting circular window at Santa Maria Novella, which is off-center relative to the evoked temple front that frames it, as well as in the missed alignments between the pilaster system above the mezzanine and the Gothic system beneath it. Here we come face to face with an experiment with the potentials of the classical language which falls short of Alberti's own theoretical criteria: the will to harmony manifest in the parts ends up revealing dissonance in the whole. What is demonstrated by this discrepancy is not only the manifest inadequacy of the humanist language as an instrument aimed at harmonizing old and new, but an even deeper aporia: new and old are able to coexist only at the price of a radical disruption of the coherence of the organism. Indeed, it almost seems as if Alberti does not use *concinnitas* to reconcile the

Gothic and humanist portions of the facade but to show that the two discourses cannot come together in any coherent way.

The Tempio Malatestiano: The Humanist Code in Crisis

A similar dynamic informs the Tempio Malatestiano in Rimini (ca. 1450), Alberti's first full-fledged architectural project (fig. 1.45). Tafuri's reading of this project is a paradigmatic instance of his approach to Alberti insofar as it exhibits salient features of his understanding of the latter's concept of architecture as representation of the *all'antica* idea. At the same time, he saw that it constituted a key moment in the development of Alberti's strategies of antiquarian reference. Yet as it turns out, this early work of Alberti was beset by so many problems, both with respect to its fundamental theoretical implications and its difficult practical realization, that it ends up registering a wider set of contradictions that Tafuri associates with a crisis of representation central to his conception of the Renaissance.

Here more context is necessary before we can examine Tafuri's interpretation of this project in greater detail. Commissioned by Sigismondo Malatesta, ruler of Rimini, the Tempio can be described as a rather modest thirteenth-century Gothic church around which the architect has wrapped a stone structure that completely encases the old building like a relic.[34] As Grafton puts it: "Alberti wrapped the old brick church of the Franciscans with a brilliantly devised shell of Istrian stone."[35] Alberti designed the main facade in the form of a Roman triumphal arch and originally intended to raise a vast dome reminiscent of the Pantheon above the crossing. The side facades contain arches supported by *columnae quadrangulae*, square columns that are segments of wall which contain niches into which sarcophagi are inserted.[36] Despite, or perhaps precisely because of, its ambitious beginning, this project was destined to remain incomplete at the time of Sigismondo's death.

The architectural envelope of the Tempio is animated by a search for organic relationships that are ambiguously combined with a "taste for the fragment" visible in its citation of the nearby

Arch of Augustus.[37] In this and in other works, particularly the Palazzo Rucellai in Florence (1446–1451), one of the clearest instances of a reliance on artifice and the idea of the masking function of the facade in Alberti's entire output, one can see, in a concrete sense, what happens when "the impulse to innovate is grafted onto the need for rule [*bisogno di regola*] left unsatisfied by a return to Vitruvius."[38] At issue in the motivation behind this impulse is what one might call Tafuri's conceptual warhorse, as far as the era of humanist architecture is concerned: the introduction, against the medieval concept of a consubstantiality of image and presence, of a system that is completely representational (*compiutamente rappresentativo*).[39]

This is the case insofar as the stylistic code deployed in the Tempio identifies the built project with an aesthetic simulation of the antique, based on the notion that imitation of ancient models will always come up short, inevitably betraying the form as well as the meaning of the models themselves. Such a strategy was bound to lead to a clash between the medieval language of the earlier church and the *all'antica* lexicon, even if the latter, in the form of a thickened shell, largely masks the former. When confronted by the discrepancy in question with the built legacy of classical antiquity, it is not simply a matter of dealing with a "lost origin": for the space it once occupied is now occupied by a new conceptualization of itself, transformed into representation, insofar as it was caught in a tug of war between rule and transgression.[40] The eventual result of all of this, which came out into the open by the third decade of the sixteenth century, is the "establishment of a code through an infinite series of exceptions."[41] The rise of this code meant that the humanist project of recovering antiquity did not frame its aims in any literal sense, but sought instead to improve upon antiquity, to rival it, to outdo it as much as possible: *to render the antique perfectly Antique*, as Tafuri phrased it, by extrapolating the latent formal idea behind the immediacy of external appearances.[42]

For Tafuri the age of humanism walked a fine line between the need for rule and the need to transgress.[43] In this context, instead of seeing the humanist project as a codification of norms, Tafuri speaks of this project in light of a curious yet crucial fact:

namely, that the need for rule which informed it was the very same force which enabled the process of transgression which generated the infinite variety of forms of the architecture of classical antiquity that Alberti, Bramante, Peruzzi, Raphael, Giulio, Michelangelo, and Palladio drew upon when producing their own universes of invention.[44] Even so, Tafuri is not so much interested in this need as in those moments of "concealed transgression" that demonstrate the potential instability of the rules themselves—something that is evident to attentive readers of Alberti's treatise on architecture no less than of his buildings, even the most "finished" and apparently self-sufficient.[45]

Characteristic of humanist architecture as a whole, this instability has roots that are already visible in the Tempio, due to the complex negotiation Alberti conducts between different variants of the classical code. It has already been noted that the Tempio reworks a specific local monument, the Arch of Augustus, in a way that is obvious, given the physical proximity of the source. This proximity is unusual in itself. For instance, Palladio did not have an analogous opportunity in the Veneto; he did not have the Pantheon in front of him when designing and building the Villa Rotonda (though there are instances in which he pays close attention to Roman provincial architecture, for example the Arco dei Borsari in Verona—even if they, too, are located at a considerable distance from his nearest projects).[46] In Alberti's use of the arch, the humanist architect transformed a Roman provincial monument that originally was erected to celebrate the Emperor Augustus. Why did he do this?

One plausible answer maintains that the Arch of Augustus was significant for the humanist in search of the local roots of the language of Roman classicism: by citing them he can connect the universality of this language to the specific sites of its emergence, showing a heightened sensitivity to provincial idioms in the process.[47] From the normative standard of Roman classicism, then, Alberti descends into the particulars of the regional dialect. There is an important theoretical lesson here: when confronted with the syntagm constituted by the *imago clipeata* and the engaged column, Alberti uses the module derived from these classical fragments to create a new exemplification of the *all'antica* discourse. In so doing, he applies the governing logic of *concinnitas* together with a high degree of sensitivity to the role of ornament. At the same time Alberti has a precise laudatory purpose: in evoking an ancient imperial source to glorify Sigismondo, the architect makes him, in effect, a new Augustus.

Significantly, this citation is part of an extended pattern of antiquarian reference which Tafuri singles out in his analysis. Alberti refers to the Arch of Augustus in Rimini to show that this city (ancient Ariminum) played a key role at the time of the founding of the Empire, insofar as this town was seen by Augustus as the perfect meeting point between the Via Flaminia and the Via Emilia: ancient memories attesting to its strategic importance consonant with the ideological program of Sigismondo.[48] In a similar vein, Alberti cites the Colosseum in the Palazzo Rucellai in Florence to show that this city, with its distinguished classical architectural culture, is the daughter of Rome; finally he cites his reading of the *templum etruscum* in Mantua, in the case of Sant'Andrea, to underscore the continuity between Etruscan origins and the city of Virgil, who sang of the Trojan Aeneas who displaced these very origins and erected a new political and social and cultural order that drew on what was partly effaced.[49] For Tafuri, this pattern of antique reference has a specific rationale: Alberti "tempered the universalism of the humanist *principia* by referring to the historicity of the sites for which his architectural projects were intended."[50] This strategy, in turn—"the attempt to situate the roots of a 'deracinated' language"—displays "significant affinities" with the contemporaneous philology of Lorenzo Valla.[51]

fig. 3.2

When designing the Tempio, Alberti's guiding theoretical idea does not propose that proportion, along with its conceptual matrix, *concinnitas*, can solve everything. Instead, he is aware of its inherent limits. Add to this the fact that a number of adverse circumstances interrupted the project—Alberti was unable to finish the building because Malatesta fell short of funds after his excommunication in 1460 and died before its completion—and one begins to sense the fragility of the entire humanist enterprise of architectural invention as Alberti conceived of it. But what Alberti did achieve is as fascinating as it is instructive, as it registers his attempt to bring the universality of the classical language down to the measure of the stylistically variegated idioms of Roman provincial architecture.

3.2 Arch of Augustus, Rimini, 27 BCE.

What does Tafuri make of all of this? Inserting the Tempio Malatestiano and Santa Maria Novella into wider cycles of *all'antica* architecture, he sees these projects as paradigmatic instances of an emerging humanist reliance upon multiple models, a practice linked to the invention and deployment of novel strategies of representation.[52] Here it is worth recalling that the Tempio was to have been completed in such a way as to glorify its patron by placing a huge cupola partly inspired by the Pantheon at its apex: a case in which one of the major precedents, and by extension the normative standard of Roman classicism, would have entered into a novel synthesis with a "minor" classical idiom, represented in this case by the Arch of Augustus. In this respect, center and periphery converge, at least in the overall design of the Tempio, if not in the built artifact or *fatto costruito*.

Other aspects of the project that Tafuri omits from his analysis, but which are pertinent to it as essential context, serve to reinforce his argument: notably the idea of recreating this church as a temple of glory for a ruler whose troubled relationship with Christianity motivated Pius II's condemnation of the Tempio as being more like a temple dedicated to pagan demons than a Christian sanctuary.[53] Pius was aware that the sarcophagi on the front facade were intended for the *condottiere* and his mistress Isotta degli Atti; he may also have been apprised of the fact that one of the side niches contained the sarcophagus of Gemisthos Pletho, a philosopher admired by Sigismondo who rejected Christianity outright in favor of a return to ancient Greek paganism.[54] Considered together, these purely cultural facets of the origin and commission of the Tempio show that Alberti's first architectural patron was unusual both for his learned fascination with antiquity and for his bold disregard of Christian morality—characteristics shared by other Renaissance princes, but not to the same degree

To be sure, the patron's desires and needs did not wholly align with the humanist culture of Alberti. This notwithstanding, it is evident that by 1453, partly due to the rhetorical abilities of the architect, agreement on the final form of the Tempio was reached. Yet this use of rhetoric, staple of humanism in an age of princes, cannot be seen as building a bridge of words over the chasm separating Alberti the itinerant intellectual from his ruthless and controversial patron; nor does it offer a sufficient *point d'appui* for speculations regarding convergent or divergent worlds of interest. Here it is worth recalling what Jakob Burckhardt's *The Civilization of the Renaissance in Italy* (1860) has to say about the ruler of Rimini, which succinctly captured what is at stake in their relationship when referring to the audacity of Sigismondo, a tyrant who buried his mistress (who only rather late in the game became his wife) right in the temple of God, which, whatever else it might signify, provides compelling evidence for the historian's hypothesis that the Italian Renaissance marks the origin of modern secular individualism.[55] Alberti's strong sense of his own individuality, underscored in myriad ways by Burckhardt, in connection with his multiple attainments that range from the most intellectual and recondite to the most corporeal and athletic, may have contributed to a certain appreciation of Sigismondo, who was not to be outdone by anyone in this regard.[56] And since Alberti could have chosen *not* to work for such a person, the fact that he did surely says something—though what precisely remains a subject of considerable debate.[57]

Tafuri cast new light on this problem by stressing the constitutive reciprocity at the heart of humanist representation.[58] In this regard the historian describes the situation linking such figures as Alberti and Sigismondo as one in which "the need to represent and the need to be represented bound artist to patron."[59] As a result, "A multiplicity of techniques of 'reciprocal instrumentalization' between artistic style and program . . . found new articulation with the rise of a 'culture of calculation.' Nonetheless this did not take place in accordance with a coincidence of their respective intentions; rather, this particular relationship assumed an essentially dialectical character, proceeding, as it were, by extremes [*per tangenze*]."[60] Caught up in the web of representation and self-representation, Alberti had little choice, when summoned by Sigismondo, but to take on the commission. What we are dealing with here is a dialectical relationship that arises *per tangenze*, an exchange that takes place through the "reciprocal instrumentalization" of program and stylistic codes, rather than in terms of any evaluation *post* or *propter hoc* of the consequences, cultural, religious, or otherwise, of the project undertaken.

It can scarcely be doubted that Sigismondo's commission involved a "tangency" of this kind, though it remains an open question whether Alberti's project compromised the architect by linking him, if only indirectly, to Sigismondo's defiance of the moral authority of the Church. What is undeniable is that the commission gave the humanist imagination of the architect free rein to transform a small Franciscan church into the site of daring experiment with the potentialities of the *all'antica* discourse. One might even surmise that the discourse itself could have proven to be subversive to the interests of the Christian religion, whose monopoly of the sacred could have been compromised by the spread of pagan forms and the revival of the classical tradition more generally. This is a possibility that Tafuri takes into account when he reminds us that Pope Nicholas V, in his so-called "political testament," proposed a program of cultural appropriation of pagan philosophical thought aimed at neutralizing any challenge to the power of the Church: "By supporting humanism and Neoplatonic culture, the learned Nicholas waged a campaign to annex mental habits that could have proven dangerous if allowed to develop autonomously."[61] In any case one can say that the Tempio was seen as a danger to the Christian religion when it was being built: the only instance of Alberti's architecture to be accorded this dubious distinction. This is evident from the aforementioned attacks of Pius II, who emphasized the subversive nature of the classical memories it stirred up.[62]

The inaugural work in Alberti's classicizing experiment was therefore not without its problematic sides. In fact, as far as the Tempio Malatestiano was concerned, not only its patron but also the classicizing idiom that the architect adopted were pervaded by uncertainties, challenges, and upheavals of all kinds (moral and ethical, not to mention religious) that provide compelling parallels with the state of crisis this work exemplifies on the level of architectural language.[63] The coordinates of this crisis are provided by the relation of theory and practice and the role of classical memories in the design of *all'antica* projects, at a key point in the emergence and transformation of the humanist discourse itself. This complex situation can be read in various ways, yet for Alberti the main issue hinges on the range of classical sources, theoretical and built, that the humanist architect might legitimately use. Is he going to apply the principles of Vitruvius? Is he prepared to rewrite and in the process displace the authority of

Vitruvius, with whom he has been aptly described as having a love-hate relationship, marked in the end more by rejection than acceptance?[64] Or is he ready to use the Arch of Augustus, which itself is a local *exemplum* that deviates in noticeable ways from the claims to a universal classicism à la Vitruvius, "sole remaining survivor of that vast shipwreck," the devouring force of time, which had swallowed up all other ancient theoretical writings on architecture that could have challenged the authority of *De architectura*?[65]

Close reading of both *De re aedificatoria* and Alberti's built projects of the same period show that he considered all of these options, some of which overlap and others of which are contradictory: the result is a flexibility of language that is inseparable from the flowering of an experimental impulse that is nonetheless integrally linked to the normative claims of rule. Such concerns assumed great importance at this point in his trajectory, at a moment when he was laying the groundwork for a theoretical project intimately bound up with his own attempt to redress the many and disturbing inadequacies he discerned in Vitruvius.[66]

Yet for Tafuri, Alberti's attempt to improve upon Vitruvius was not a total success either, since it was compromised in a number of ways that have a specific bearing on his reading of the Tempio Malatestiano. Situating the Tempio against the background of the scission between Alberti's *De re aedificatoria*, whose composition was under way in the early 1450s just as this project was being built, and his darkly pessimistic literary writings of the early 1440s, including the *Intercoenales* and *Momus* (1450), Tafuri points out the inconsistencies in Alberti's approach which are at once the result of a crisis in the conception of disciplinary rationality upheld in his treatise and the numerous challenges presented by the building process. "Architecture appears as the imposition of an order known to be fallible," he writes in 1979, "on a life which explodes in nightmarish forms"—the very same forms that Tafuri noted in the literary texts just mentioned. He then asks, in an especially pregnant sentence, "Does all this help to understand the 'limitation' which Alberti imposes on his architectonic objects in an ungovernable city, and the tangible criticism which stunts works like the Tempio Malatestiano and San Sebastiano in Mantua?"[67]

It is hard to know exactly what Tafuri is referring to when he speaks of "tangible criticism," a phrase that is so cryptic as to merit comparison to the sibylline obscurity of Alberti's own emblem of the flying eye. Perhaps it is his intention to say that Alberti equated architecture with criticism at some level: if this is indeed the case, then the *all'antica* language that he was fashioning might be seen as a tangible, material, and constructed critique of the medieval core that it encases. On the other hand, it does seem that in speaking of an "ungovernable city" he is alluding, if only obliquely, to the political and religious rebelliousness of Alberti's first major architectural patron, Sigismondo Malatesta. As to the reference to "limitation," Tafuri might be referring to the fact that Alberti had to preserve as well as partly hide the earlier medieval structure that would end up being largely (but not entirely) sheathed within his classicizing shell. The reference to San Sebastiano, a botched project if there ever was one, at least as far as Alberti's trajectory is concerned, only completes the image of an architecture in crisis, from the point of view both of the application of a fallible theory that does not live up to its own aspirations to total rationality, and of the vicissitudes of practice.[68]

This theme was touched upon a decade earlier, albeit in slightly different form, when Tafuri pointed out that by leaving the completion of the nave of the Tempio Malatestiano to Matteo de' Pasti, "proposing to superimpose on the linguistic *pastiche* of his collaborator the projected but not realized vast dome" of the church, Alberti's goals are by no means as linear and autonomous as those of his precursor Brunelleschi.[69] Alberti thus appears as a figure who is uncertain about how to proceed when faced by practical exigences linked to the *cantiere* of the Tempio no less than by theoretical problems raised by the project, suspended between a deficient rationality in his own approach and a willingness to endorse the medieval preexistences and the linguistically hybrid, provisional solutions of de' Pasti.

Alberti and Nicholas V: The Problem of the Urban Plan of Rome

For Tafuri, Alberti's penchant for artifice, manifest in the different idioms adopted in his projects in Rimini, Florence, and Mantua, paved the way for the sophisticated strategies of representation employed by his early sixteenth-century followers, Raphael and Giulio in particular. It was the latter who, in the Palazzo Te in Mantua, would end up making "paradoxical use of *concinnitas*" by deploying irregular rhythms, broken architraves, clashing uses of the orders, and a generalized poetics of the fragment to bring out a tragic (or tragicomic) isolation of moments of harmony.[70] This point is brought home with special force when Tafuri equates the image of a silent architecture with the caesura Alberti discerned in the discipline's metaphysical grounding. Here I will quote the entire paragraph in which Tafuri analyzed the Tempio Malatestiano in relation to San Sebastiano, as cited previously, in order to provide a better sense of what he intended to convey regarding the subversive nature of Alberti's theoretical contribution to the discipline: "Architecture appears as the imposition of an order known to be fallible, on a life which explodes in nightmarish forms. Does all this help us to understand the meaning of the 'limitation' which Alberti imposed on his architectonic objects within an uncontrollable city, and the tangible criticism which stunts works like the Tempio Malatestiano or San Sebastiano in Mantua? It is certain that when Alberti imposes it on himself *not to make architecture speak*, he slowly and secretly undermines the relationship between practice and theory existing about the middle of the fifteenth century."[71]

These considerations bring us to the threshold between the *res aedificatoria* and the city: a contested border whose problematic nature is self-evident. It is only by entering this terrain that we may approach the question of Alberti's role in the "plan" for Rome initiated, and at least partly executed (or so it has been claimed), by Pope Nicholas V.[72] Although this is not the place for an extensive discussion of the Nicoline "plan" (which may not have existed in any case), we may still take note of one of the arguments that Tafuri advanced in his analysis of the so-called *piano Nicolino*: namely, that even if Alberti did assume the role of humanist counselor to the Pope, certain works that have traditionally been seen as key parts of the urban plan, such as the Nicoline Fontana di Trevi, are so manifestly mediocre as to suggest that Alberti had no hand in their design.[73]

Anthony Grafton has identified the historiographical demolition operation that Tafuri accomplished with regard to

Alberti and Nicholas as a *tour de force* of scholarship. After careful evaluation of the available evidence, both textual and architectural, Tafuri picks apart the scholarly assumptions that have conditioned reconstructions of the Nicoline "plan" until almost nothing is left.[74] In particular Tafuri cites passages from *De re aedificatoria* that cite the Neronian mania for the colossal and the Vitruvian account of Dinocrates as evidence that Alberti could neither have devised nor approved of Nicholas's ambitious projects for the Borgo or St. Peter's.[75] These passages, read in conjunction with a text by the civic humanist Matteo Palmieri in which Alberti is said to have counseled Nicholas not to proceed further on his program of works aimed at renovating St. Peter's, rightly earn Grafton's praise.[76]

This is the case even if the American historian has more than one reservation about Tafuri's redimensioning of Alberti's role in Nicoline Rome, given the fact that the critique in *Momus* is directed not only at the all-powerful gods but at the decidedly more vulnerable figure of Momus himself.[77] It does not add to the weight of these reservations, however, that Tafuri suggests, after painstaking reconstruction of the vicissitudes surrounding Alberti's "no" with regard to his role as counselor on urban and architectural matters, that the relationship between Alberti and Nicholas was an education in aesthetics, and at the same time an education in limits.[78] Nor does it come as much of a surprise either to him or to us that, with regard to Alberti's "yes"—namely, the positive content deposited within, and indeed the very fact of having written, the *De re aedificatoria* itself—papal Rome in Nicholas's time was in no position, either intellectually or politically, to properly receive or even to understand what Tafuri calls the "theoretical 'quantum leap' in the conception of architecture" brought about by the treatise.[79] In any case it is hardly necessary for our present purposes to go into the finer points of the scholarly controversy regarding Alberti's possible role as humanist advisor to Nicholas. Such hypotheses—which have been debated *ad infinitum* in the scholarly literature since Georg Dehio inaugurated the investigation of this area of Alberti studies in the late nineteenth century—are simply not relevant to the questions at hand.[80]

At this point, the question to ask is not whether Alberti applied his urban theories to an actual city (Rome) under the control of a particularly ambitious humanist pope (Nicholas V), but whether the reflection on the limits of architecture elaborated in his treatise and built works can help us iron out the difficulties surrounding the nature and extent of the Nicoline "plan." The most persuasive answer, according to Tafuri—and this point is subtler than it might seem—is that Alberti would likely have refused to accede to the desires of Nicholas. This is because Alberti's theoretical attitude toward the dyad architecture/urban space and the related dialectic between the architectural project and the preexisting realities of the city would have justified such a refusal. Tafuri points out that we cannot yet speak of urbanism since that is a nineteenth-century conception, often applied arbitrarily to earlier eras, with the effect of making scholars and others think that someone like Nicholas, along with Alberti, could have had a "master plan": a hypothesis, or rather the ideological distortion of a hypothesis, about which Tafuri expresses an extreme skepticism.[81]

In forging links in a chain that are largely negative, Tafuri's suggestion that it would have been extremely unlikely for Alberti to have acted as a humanist advisor encouraging Nicholas to carry out a master plan for Rome marks a significant shift in our conception of Alberti. What stands out in Tafuri's approach to this problem is the political side of his argument: since, in the *De Porcaria coniuratione* (1453), an account of Stefano Porcari's plot to overthrow Nicholas, Alberti inserted long speeches that were anti-authoritarian and pro-republican in character, Tafuri infers that the humanist intellectual, despite his professional role in the curia as *abbreviatore apostolico*, a kind of humanist secretary charged with writing papal briefs and speeches, put his own political ideas in the mouth of Porcari himself, and would therefore have opposed any architectural and/or urban expansion of papal power.[82]

To a certain extent, Alberti's imposition of limits on *techne* is bound up with a critique of what Foucault called a "political technology" when referring to schemes of social control aimed at dominating urban space (a theme Tafuri addressed when discussing the urban strategies adopted by Julius II and Leo X).[83] The principal evidence for this argument cannot be found in the text itself but in the fact that Alberti expressed perplexity that he was allowed to remain in the Eternal City so that he could write the history of the plot and its exposure.[84] Here the Pope's aim was to remind all who might have initially thought otherwise that rebellion was not worth the price.[85] Alberti would thus have been seen as "winnable" from the point of view of the authoritarian Nicholas, as well as useful, despite, or perhaps precisely because of, the fact that he was an effectively isolated presence in the papal court, both politically and intellectually.[86]

Yet as usually is the case with Tafuri, more profound conceptual and theoretical problems are at stake. These can be seen in his reading of the structure of negation that characterizes Albertian irony in a number of literary texts including *De iciarchia*, *Intercoenales*, *Theogenius*, and *Momus*.[87] In addition to offering ample evidence of a "dark" Alberti, these writings allow us to trace the dialectic between architecture and politics that so strongly marks his thought. Furthermore, these "minor" works of Alberti are used to reframe and, in many cases, to undermine the theses put forward in *De re aedificatoria*, which Alberti may or may not have written expressly for Nicholas V in order to recommend himself as a sort of counselor-at-large on architectural and urban problems.[88] At any rate Tafuri's incisive observations in this respect are informed by a pervasive sense of the tragic limitations of mortal existence and the futility of human striving—themes already touched on in "Discordant Harmony from Alberti to Zuccari," where they serve to fill out the picture of a deeply pessimistic Alberti, devoid of trust both in the world of men and in nature.[89] This was the inevitable corollary of Tafuri's vision of Alberti's presumed harmonicism as a *fable convenue*, and ultimately as a historiographical relic.

What all of this shows, beyond the historian's immediate purpose of taking Garin's approach in new directions, is that it is characteristic of Tafuri, when dealing with Alberti's architecture, to focus on situations in which the latter enters into dialogue with rhetoric and literary expression. This in turn provides a conducive matrix for new readings of Alberti's multifaceted achievement and often inscrutable texts: a procedure that is justified by the fact that Alberti was first and foremost a literary and oratorical expert, a humanist in the Quattrocento sense, before turning to architecture in the late 1440s.[90]

Two related themes stand out in Tafuri's discussion of Alberti and Nicholas: the deliberate assault on harmonic analogism and the critical affinity that Tafuri discerns between Alberti's stance and that of Momus, the ironic, antiauthoritarian rebel. Tafuri goes so far as to suggest that the figure of Momus is a portrayal of Alberti himself.[91] To substantiate both claims, Tafuri cites passages from *De re aedificatoria* that read like determinate reversals of other parts of the text that Wittkower selected to demonstrate the primacy of Alberti's harmonic analogism. "When discussing the form of the circle, Alberti merely describes it as prevalent, without making any metaphysical claims for this form whatsoever. Among the examples of circularity, including the terrestrial globe, stars, and trees, he refers to animals *eorumque nidificationes* (and their nests).[92] In his apology for hexagonal forms, Alberti calls attention to the example of beehives. . . . In Book 9 he dispassionately recalls philosophical justifications mixed with others deriving from superstitions of the most various kinds, concerning the properties of number."[93] At this point, however, the tone Alberti adopts when listing the orifices of animals as a guide to the number of openings a building should have leaves us with little doubt as to the pervasive irony of his intentions.[94] Moreover, Alberti insists that the origin of music—and here one recalls the importance of the theory of musical harmonics in Neoplatonic speculation—is found in the buzzing of flies.[95] Thus an elevated Pythagorean theme that entered directly into Platonic philosophy and from there into Neoplatonic speculation is rendered ridiculous by a *reductio ad absurdum*. It comes as no surprise, then, that Tafuri speaks of Alberti in this vein as expressing a *will to desacralize* Pythagorean musical doctrine, and, together with these, a certain hostility toward the Pythagorean harmonic concepts in Renaissance Neoplatonism.[96]

It goes without saying that such caustic naturalism does not sit well with Wittkower's picture of Alberti as a convinced Neoplatonist who based his theory of architecture on nature's pervasive harmonic relationships. Here we can be more specific. Tafuri does not argue that Alberti was unfamiliar with Neoplatonic thought—the fact that he did know it was a point that Wittkower and Tafuri agreed upon to some extent—but that his attitude toward it was anything but univocal and affirming, as Wittkower had stated.[97] In other words: Wittkower unjustly assumed that Alberti's knowledge of Neoplatonic harmonicism (and of its Pythagorean substrate in particular) implied Alberti's full-throated endorsement of this philosophical tendency (something that, despite the obvious strengths of Wittkower's argument in other respects, he asserts without sufficient evidence).[98] Such knowledge—part of a much wider set of philosophical ideas that attracted Alberti's interest over the course of his long career—was in any case simply not as important for him as Wittkower would have us believe.[99]

In this regard it is revealing that Tafuri stresses, in marked contrast to Wittkower, the dissonant side of the Albertian universe. This aspect of Alberti becomes particularly evident when taking up the challenge of interpreting *Momus*, a complex text in which the eponymous protagonist mocks Jupiter's plan to rebuild heaven, a subtle critique, perhaps, of Nicholas's strategies for rebuilding Rome. What is more, Tafuri points to a passage in Book 2 of *De re aedificatoria* in which Alberti criticizes unrestrained *hybris* in its diverse manifestations, including the Neronian mania for colossal constructions and the vain attempts to tunnel through mountains.[100] There is also a passage in *Libri della famiglia* in which Alberti speaks of the futility of felling huge numbers of trees merely to create roofs over our heads; one also recalls the observation, put forth in *Theogenius*, that animals are content with what they find, unlike man, the only animal who is continually searching for new things, and in so doing violates and destroys them—a text that reaches heights of anguish and tension rarely equaled in his other writings, except perhaps for the *Profugiorum ab aerumna Libri III*, some of the *Intercoenales*, and certain passages portraying both mockery and the infinite capacity for cruelty of both humans and the gods in *Momus*.[101]

Whereas Alberti's architecture has often been understood in light of the *De re aedificatoria*, the links between his built works and his literary texts have rarely been explored in detail. The same can be said, to some extent, of the interconnections between his literary texts and his theoretical works, even if, since Tafuri's time, new readings have begun to change our understanding of these relationships. Although many scholars from Burckhardt onward have considerably enriched their approaches to Alberti's built projects by readings of his theoretical writings, very few until Tafuri had used his literary production to cast new light on his architecture—not even Garin, who tended to concentrate on the literary production alone. Tafuri stands out in this regard: he was, if not the first, then certainly among the most original and penetrating interpreters of the complex, at times troubled relationship between Alberti *architetto, teorico e letterato*.

From the Limits of *Techne* to the Power of Beauty

Taken together, the diverse pieces of evidence that Tafuri drew from Alberti's literary texts and built projects add up to a picture of a deeply reflective, disenchanted thinker who sought to impose order on the chaotic world around him, especially the urban world, through architecture, while calling for the imposition of ethical limits on *techne*. And it is at this precise point that the aesthetic and the ethical dimensions of Alberti's universe intersect, with consequences that are as unexpected as they are revealing. This is the case insofar as the power unleashed by technical rationality is an integral part of the human rapaciousness that Alberti singles out for criticism, serving as a privileged mode of instrumentality aimed at dominating nature.

Here a passage stands out from the *Theogenius*, a text that Tafuri saw as typical of the radical pessimism pervading Albertian thought. This work maintains that man is a wolf to others, hostile to all created things.[102] In view of these and similar statements, it is clear that, in this text, harmony between man and his fellow men, and between man and nature, if possible at all, can only exist as a provisional condition, through the use of restraint and measure, which stand out against the unbridled will to dominate all that exists. It is worth noting here that measure (*misura*), a significant aspect of Platonic, Neoplatonic, and Pythagorean thought, is also a defining characteristic of the Stoic ideal of self-conquest.[103] Key moments in Alberti's literary writings valorize self-control over other forms of control of nature and men, in open contradiction to the praise of technological might elaborated in

Book 1 of *De re aedificatoria*, in connection with the definition of the tasks and capacities of the architect.[104] Tafuri does not try to paper over this inconsistency, nor does he choose to ignore it. Instead he uses the fissures in Alberti's theoretical reflection on the power of *techne* as an object lesson in the aporias of humanist thought. If at the beginning of *Interpreting the Renaissance* Tafuri discerned the workings of *hybris* moving just beneath the irenic claims of humanism, he singles out Alberti as performing an exceptional role in denouncing just this kind of arrogance in the field of architecture.[105]

In the opening pages of *Interpreting the Renaissance*, Tafuri cites Martin Heidegger's "The Question Concerning Technology" (1954), an essay combining a trenchant critique of technology with a vision of modernity based on the triumph of the principle of representation in the "world epoch placed in an image."[106] This work suggested certain directions of argument to Tafuri with reference to the Renaissance perspective panels and the airless urban spaces depicted in the *studioli* in Urbino and Gubbio, in which the historian discerns nothing less than a "terroristic effect."[107] In particular, Heidegger's reflections inspired Tafuri's suggestion that this totalizing—and overwhelming—mode of representation coincides with the *hybris* that Alberti denounces in *Momus* and in certain passages in *De re aedificatoria*. To be sure, Tafuri is by no means in complete agreement with Heidegger, particularly when asserting that the link established by the German philosopher between the will to power and Western technology "has its problematic sides," and moreover does not entirely apply to Renaissance Venice, where resistances and contradictions to the rise of *techne* were no trivial matter, but constituted productive factors in their own right (paradoxically enough) from the point of view of the mentalities and *imaginaire* of the city in question.[108]

Of equal importance in this regard are the writings of Tafuri's friend the philosopher Massimo Cacciari, from whom Tafuri took the idea of Promethean guilt concerning the theft of fire. In connection with this one must also consider the mythic origins in Western culture of the guilt complex linked with technology's domination of nature, which holds that the foundation of *techne* is not in *techne* itself.[109] From this, Tafuri, who calls this intuition of Cacciari's "profound," infers that not only fire, *ab illo tempore*, but "the foundation has itself been stolen."[110] Here we may observe, beyond any question concerning technology, a parallel, not noted by Tafuri himself, between the lost origin of the classical referent of the *all'antica* language and the stolen foundation of Promethean technology. Thus the original sin regarding technology and its corollary, the domination of nature, resides in the absolutization of *techne* which covers over this theft of foundations, both as far as technology is concerned, in *mythic* terms, and as far as architecture is concerned, in purely *conceptual* terms.

As Tafuri puts it, "a *techne* sure of its own foundations is oblivious of the originary crime": for this reason Alberti, who would place limits on the use of technical instrumentality in general, can be said to express, if only between the lines of his treatise, a profound insecurity concerning the scope and purpose of this very instrumentality.[111] Tafuri has the following to say about this particular instance of ethical reflection: "Only a humanist able to orient himself in multiple fields of knowledge can recognize the necessity of knowing oneself through one's limits: an awareness permitted by *techne*. *Hybris*, which appears in the Promethean claim to transform the part into the whole, can be mastered by engaging in a maieutics of the limit."[112] This leads to an unambiguous conception of the *virtù* of the architect within Alberti's mental universe: "The 'virtuous' architect is such because he transcends the bestiality of human nature.... The cult of the limit... gives way to the acceptance—voluntary, unfounded, tragic—of this ethical stance. It is no accident that the hermetic architectural objects created by Alberti display their own desperate solitude."[113] Such is Tafuri's view, *in nuce*, of the architectural ethics and its inextricable connection to what one could call a formal aesthetics of solitude in Alberti.

In light of the preceding, one can say that, for Alberti, it is not *techne* but *concinnitas* that offers a compelling argument for the legitimacy of techniques of design, representation, and "constructed representation," insofar as it confers a unifying dimension on these techniques. This is because, more than anything else, *concinnitas* does not involve the peremptory and unjustified project of turning the part into the whole but the meticulous and justified effort to coordinate parts with each other with an eye to the coherence of the greater whole they help bring about. Here the pertinent area that Alberti is drawing upon is not technology but rhetoric.[114] The term *concinnitas*, of Ciceronian provenance, can be translated as a harmony or elegance of design, especially of literary style, in the adaptation of parts to a whole or to each other, a harmony that was for Alberti eminently suitable, and easily transferable, as a regulative principle for architecture. In its capacity as an ideal of harmonic coherence linking architecture to the cosmos (albeit in ways that are not reducible to Wittkower's Neoplatonic reading), it simultaneously evokes, yet also supersedes, the Vitruvian notion of *symmetria partium* and the Ciceronian concept of rhetorical parallelism, in which form and content attain equilibrium.[115]

In giving architecture a definitive correspondence of parts so that nothing can be added or removed without detriment to the whole, the inviolable coherence that *concinnitas* secures for the work confers upon the realized project a sort of apotropaic power. Moving within the coordinates laid down by this concept, Alberti argued that architecture, among all the arts, is the one best suited to withstand the corrosive force of time: in his view, by drawing upon the principles of *concinnitas* and *finitio*, the built project can attain a level of beauty that can shield itself from the ravages of time and the fury of the barbarian. As a result, these categories and the aesthetic qualities associated with them "exert a *weak power*. In other words, quality is a deterrent."[116] Alberti was the first to recognize the wellsprings of this power by working backward from its effects: in so doing, he was also the earliest of all fifteenth-century architect-theorists to elaborate a concept of architectural "fortitude" that proposed beauty as an unexpected source of resistance, or unique counterforce to the destabilizing powers of time and the seemingly limitless human potential for violence, rapaciousness, and destructive folly.[117]

Fifteenth-Century Receptions of Alberti: Giuliano da Sangallo and Francesco di Giorgio

Assessments of other kinds of weakness and strength are, of course, key to the political dimension of Alberti's dual experience as humanist and architect. As far as the early reception of Alberti's architectural theory is concerned, specific political implications become evident in two fifteenth-century projects, one realized, the other not, by Giuliano da Sangallo. Both figure prominently in Tafuri's discussion of the Albertian elements in the work of this architect. The first is for an unbuilt palace near Via Laura for the Medici; the second is the Medici villa at Poggio a Caiano.[118] The Medici found it prudent not to build such a vast palace, which would have rivaled antiquity in its control of space and its menacing presence in the city, possibly reflecting Alberti's partly ironic, partly serious proposals in Book 9 of *De re aedificatoria* regarding the typological characteristics and strategic siting of the tyrant's palace.[119] Like Alberti's idealized description of the latter, the Via Laura palace would have been immense in scale and built against the city walls, as part of its fortifications, so as to instill fear in the citizens. For Alberti, who in this respect anticipates Machiavelli, the advice regarding a princely strategy aimed at the domination of urban space and civic life would appear to have a satirical dimension.[120]

The idea of building a fortified palace against the city walls was ultimately rejected: instead, the Medici undertook projects of villa architecture that were as ambitious as they were refined.[121] Tafuri points out that in so doing, the Medici could indulge their taste for grandeur in the countryside, as opposed to the city, both in the case of Poggio a Caiano outside Florence and of Villa Madama outside Rome.[122] At Poggio a Caiano, Giuliano follows Alberti's strictures regarding monumental civic building, most notably with regard to the *templum*, a classicizing term he uses to designate the church. According to Alberti, this type of building, marked by a *dignitas* that sets it above other structures, should be raised on a plinth, elevating it above the "rest of the city"—"a caetero Urbis," as he puts it.[123] Giuliano's transposition of a convention usually reserved for sacred buildings to the secular villa type only makes the innovative character of this villa stand out all the more, even as it reflects, in a highly original way, Alberti's observation in Book 9 that the ornament of the villa is permitted a greater margin of license that is denied to the urban residence.[124]

Yet Giuliano does not simply rely on this aspect of Alberti's theory: in his conspicuous insertion of a temple front into the body of the villa, a secular structure dedicated to humanist *otium*, he also prefigures and to some extent makes possible Palladio's typological *ars combinatoria* and the epochal renewal of the villa that resulted from it. What is more, at Poggio a Caiano Giuliano went farther in the direction of radical typological transposition than Alberti ever did, even if Alberti had used Roman triumphal arch motifs, which are typological elements in themselves, as a means of radically reinventing the design of church facades in four separate instances: Tempio Malatestiano, Santa Maria Novella, San Sebastiano, and Sant'Andrea. In Giuliano's case the building is located in the countryside, so no envy could be stirred up among the urban citizenry (according to Vasari, Brunelleschi's project for a grandiose urban palace for the Medici was rejected by Cosimo on the grounds that "envy is a flower that should not be watered").[125] Giuliano da Sangallo's villa is thereby ennobled, rendered autonomous, and isolated in a way that reworks Albertian theory and practice, inflecting it in a direction that is highly original. In this regard Giuliano approached Alberti in much the same way as Alberti approached antiquity: with an attitude of free invention.

A similar freedom in the handling of Albertian concepts and motifs can be seen in Francesco di Giorgio's design for the cloister of the monastery church of San Bernardino (1474), which reworks the sides of the Tempio Malatestiano with its *columnae quadrangulae* in a powerful, almost elemental way, using local brick-and-mortar construction. A comparable treatment is found in the exterior of the superimposed arcades of the Convent of Santa Chiara in Urbino by the same architect. It is for this reason that Tafuri characterizes the architect's formal language as "albertianamente antialbertiano."[126]

Sixteenth-Century Receptions of Alberti: Giulio Romano, Palladio, Barbaro

After Francesco di Giorgio, the next figure who responded in a highly inventive way to Alberti was Raphael. In a powerful reading, Tafuri showed how Raphael uses *concinnitas* with great *disinvoltura* in the Villa Madama (1518–1525) by balancing symmetrical and asymmetrical elements and using axialities grounded in Albertian practice and theory even as they move beyond his example.[127] Remaining for the moment in the circle of Raphael's disciples as we enter the sixteenth century, one of the more remarkable instances of using Alberti to go beyond Alberti can be seen in the portion of this same project by the young Giulio Romano. On the valley facade of the villa the basic elements of the grammar of architecture, i.e., the wall and column, fade into each other: the pilasters flanking the thermal window progressively vanish into the wall mass. This generates an austere effect that makes Alberti's near-fusion of these same elements on the facade of Sant'Andrea seem much less radical by comparison.[128] In so doing, the young Giulio all but strips the column—for Alberti, the chief ornament of architecture—of its ornamental function. This strategy clearly distinguishes Giulio's contribution to Villa Madama from other works of the same period, and in the same Roman milieu, such as Raphael's Palazzo Branconio dell'Aquila (c. 1518–1520), in whose design intricate forms of rhetorical excess figure prominently.[129]

But developments that were even more unexpected marked the trajectory of Giulio. Attaining his mature style in the Palazzo Te, this daring architect/artist recuperates the entire apparatus of *columnatio*, albeit with a powerful dose of irony: this work, more than any other of its time, exhibits a whole series of ludic and grotesque uses of the orders, and along with this a radical conception of texture, ornament, and surface, that registers, in an exceptionally vivid way, an open-minded approach to the potentials of Albertian *concinnitas*. At Palazzo Te, dissonance is used as an ironic means of achieving a unique equilibrium between rule and license, balancing out the overall organism to create a seriocomic effect. Consequently, at this point in his trajectory Giulio issues a profound challenge to the inherited certitudes of the humanist discourse. So much so that, as already seen, Tafuri speaks of a paradoxical use of *concinnitas*, as if the Alberti of *Momus*, inventive author of the adventures of the subversive god of criticism, and the Alberti of *De re aedificatoria*, erudite guarantor of theoretical and practical knowledge, had converged in a single figure.[130] Giulio's extensive use of simulated materials, deployed to give the impression of marble in both finished and rough states, together with his actualization of the conceit that the building can paradoxically outlast the effects of time by simulating a ruin (e.g., the slipped triglyphs in the Palazzo Te *cortile*) or the unfinished (as in the entryway vestibule), register a complex approach that is in some ways Albertian in spirit, albeit transposed to a different stylistic register and exhibiting a wider range of syntactical variability than any of Alberti's formal experiments.

Yet it is in his analysis of Palladio, not only of Giulio, that Tafuri's reading of Alberti's sixteenth-century reception broke new ground. Indeed Tafuri's approach to the Palladio/Alberti nexus effects a shift of emphasis that is nothing less than momentous: instead of having to deal with a new humanist part that ends up being compromised by an older medieval whole, a situation in which the classical norms are thrown into crisis as in Santa Maria Novella, Palladio overcame this problem by proposing a *built realization of the norm*, the paradigm of a modern language based on the antique but precluding any literal imitation. This approach renders inoperative any ambiguous coexistence between modern intervention and medieval residues as seen for instance in Santa Maria Novella, and, in a different sense, in the Tempio Malatestiano, through a more general reworking of stylistic codes, privileging the extrapolation of the antique into the present by means of a new thematization of *techne* and *machinatio*.

Tafuri links this reading of technical norms to the modern phenomenon of time-saving devices, thereby drawing an unexpected connection between architecture and different ways of dealing with time, as a key to the attempt to overcome human finitude. He points out that the strategies for countering the corrosive effect of time are not primarily obtained through *machinatio*, but through the creation of new possibilities for artistic (and architectural) fame. In this regard Tafuri compares Daniele Barbaro's concept of *techne* to Alberti's, and at first glance the two seem to be similar in certain respects.[131] However, Tafuri argues that one should not underestimate the differences. For Alberti, *techne* has intrinsic limits that correspond, if only obliquely, to the formal limits imposed by *finitio* on projects ordered according to the norm of *concinnitas*. Barbaro does away with the first of these limits and "thus steps over the strict boundary Alberti placed upon human inquiry."[132] In a manner consonant with this surpassing of an epistemic threshold, *machinatio*, to the extent that it enters into strictly architectural parameters, enables the architect and humanist technician to "save time," to create a charmed circle in which the ravages of mortality and the inexorable forces of decay could be suspended, if only provisionally. As Tafuri put it, speaking of Barbaro's theoretical insight, "the force of the norm is directly proportional to the *project of controlling time* that is contained in technical practices," among which one must emphatically include architecture.[133]

Barbaro's irenic position, partly Platonic in its emphasis on *eidos*, partly Aristotelian in its thematization of *techne*, made the intersection of diverse spatial and temporal imperatives possible in ways that were of great benefit to the architectural discipline.[134] What stands out here is the fact that Barbaro's conception of these theoretical problems radicalized, and in a certain way overcame, Alberti's ambivalent attitude toward *techne*, enabling the discovery of a new means of controlling the effects of the passage of time: in the case of *techne*, it is the labor- and time-saving device that fulfills this purpose; in the case of architecture, it is *virtù*, which consists in the application of harmonic principles that result in buildings that confer eternal fame on their creators.[135] In this respect, for Barbaro the formal language of architecture becomes both a technical arena of unforeseen power and a singular guarantor of fame.[136] Both Barbaro and Palladio maintained that fame, the result of virtue exercised under the most challenging circumstances, is able to overcome fortune, even if the theoretical and practical ensembles of knowledge that link architecture to *techne* intersect only at the level of representation which, to a large degree, is dependent on the *ingenium* and the *ars* of the architect.[137] Here we do not need to be reminded that *virtù*, for Palladio as well as for Barbaro, is a quality that pertains to those who know when to adhere to the rules and when to suspend them: when to adopt, instead, rule's complementary antithesis, the power of *invenzione*.

These insights inform *Venezia e il Rinascimento* (1985), a study which, along with the coauthored volume *L'armonia e i conflitti* (1983), marks the real flowering of Tafuri's polycentric method, in response to Carlo Ginzburg's microhistory.[138] If, in 1968 and 1969, Tafuri stressed the typological variability and formal inventiveness of Palladio's villas, by 1985 he had already shifted his priorities, choosing to overlook the openness of the villas in favor of an emphasis on how the self-enclosed rationality of the contours and proportions of the Venetian churches separates them from the rest of the urban context.[139] In this respect, just as his shift of focus from the city to the countryside served to accentuate the divergences between Palladio and Alberti, the reverse journey ended up revealing where they converged on the formal level both with reference to the question of *techne* and apart from it. For Palladio, the force of normative principle, having already assimilated Alberti's theoretical message, becomes at once more sure of itself and more specific in its thematizations: by generating innumerable variations on an underlying geometric schema, Palladio's new idea of rule can focus more sharply on the problem of the villa type, and thus becomes capable of producing a wider variety of architectural forms and functional spaces than those generated by the Albertian synthesis of *numerus*, *finitio*, and *concinnitas*. In a sense, Palladio uses the villa to rewrite all of architecture, whereas no such power of typological concentration ever yielded the same spectrum of invention in Alberti—not even in his most inventive approaches to the problems posed by ecclesiastical architecture.

Wielding the potent instrument of his typological approach, Palladio managed to be at once more focused and more universal than Alberti.[140] In consequence, Palladio's conception of the norm, flexible where Vitruvius's was rigid, expresses his newfound confidence in the power of *regola* on the one hand by allowing for infinite typological variability, and on the other by imbuing both the theory and practice of type with a novel propensity to extrapolate new forms of order from the malleable syntax. As a result, the limits of type and those of invention coincide, possibly for the first time in the history of architecture. Just as the constantly reinvented typological matrix conquers space, it also wins a victory over time.[141] In the end, it would seem that Palladio ends up being more internally consistent than Alberti: he more effectively fuses interior and exterior, space and facade, the logic of type and that of form and structure. Yet since the present condition of architecture is arguably marked by a considerable hybridity of codes, perhaps Alberti, in his preference for linguistic contaminations, has more to teach us than Palladio. At the same time Tafuri showed the extent to which Alberti was a paradoxical figure who, guided by a novel idea of measure, still tried to conquer entire fields of art and knowledge in ways that were *hors mesure*: so much so that one is compelled to acknowledge the tacit presence of a barrier dividing his architectural cosmos from that of Palladio, who harbored no such ambitions.

Conclusion

Kurt W. Forster once observed that every era discovers its own Palladio.[142] The same can be said of Alberti. Here it is worth recalling that one of the most characteristic features of Palladio's architecture, the typological *ars combinatoria* animating his approach to the villa, marks the point where he diverges most sharply from Alberti. Tafuri was, in fact, only partly correct when he maintained that those architects who assimilated Alberti's principles betrayed them by adopting simplified understandings of his architectural theory: for with Palladio it is clear that, building on Alberti, after having absorbed his thought he was able to move beyond, rather than to betray, his illustrious precursor.

When dealing with these and similar problems Tafuri observed that the historian's task is not to "recombine fragments." "Nor is it legitimate," he adds, "for the historian to identify with the victors—a vice that complements the apologia for present-day conditions that is, lamentably, still quite active."[143] If the second part of this admonition can only tenuously be connected to Alberti (if at all), the first assumes a specific meaning in Alberti's case, much of whose most characteristic and enduring work, paradoxically enough, is fragmentary and incomplete. But beyond any material deficiencies or fortuitous incompleteness, Alberti's fractured achievement stands out against the horizon of the humanist era as an enigmatic presence, an endlessly renewed paradox, both for the architects and readers of his own time and for us. This is not only because, as his emblem of the flying eye indicates, he took pleasure in allegories and oblique modes of expression, but also because of deeper reasons that speak to the intimate connection between his aesthetic and his ethical thought, mediated by the notion of an inner integrity or wholeness, the result of *concinnitas*, that is as hard to achieve as it is powerful to behold.[144] This, too, did not escape Tafuri: by tracing Alberti's various receptions from the beginning of that era to its end, the Italian historian delineated the essential contours of what Alberti meant to his contemporaries and to his heirs, from Francesco di Giorgio to Palladio, as well as how he was misunderstood by them—above all by referring to an ideal of wholeness, but also through an awareness of the ironic power of *fortuna*, as much of what Alberti built was not whole and never will be.

Curiously, the fact that Alberti was obsessed with wholeness, with the ideal of *concinnitas* and all that it entailed in terms of coherence, beauty, and totality, made Tafuri pay close attention to the fissures, cracks, the overall fragmentation, and ultimately to the pervasive sense of crisis that traverses the Albertian edifice. Here it is worth noting that, in the historiography on Alberti, Tafuri is in fact the only scholar—Garin included—to have consistently taken up this phenomenon of crisis in all of its manifestations, particularly in connection with the themes of the *fragment* and the *mask*, and to have made it the keynote of his approach. These themes, moreover, reveal the problematic nature of any attempt to represent the perfection of classical order, the solitude that extends from the restless intellectual subject to the isolated architectural object, the ceaseless experiment with language driven by transgression and license, and the disparate linguistic codes that Alberti was compelled to work with both over the course of his career and often within the same project. It is from reflection on these different yet related aspects of Alberti that his significance became most evident to Tafuri, who teased out the implications of the nexus of rule and infraction in the contribution of this pivotal figure while using them as a paradigm for understanding the inner dynamics of the humanist language: "Perhaps, after having penetrated to a realm beyond every absolute law—to a place where the 'spirit of destruction' acquires a constructive vocation—does it become at all possible to examine the spirit of the law."[145]

From this he understood, early on, that the meaning of rules becomes most explicit when they are broken. Tafuri discovered this "semiosis of infraction" by probing the hidden links between *tradire* (to pass down) and *tradere* (to betray), demonstrating the constitutive bond between tradition and the new that arises out of the violation of rules evident at every phase of Alberti's life and work.[146] Fundamental to any understanding of Alberti, who epitomized this balance between *regola* and *licenza*, this bond sheds light on his inaugural role within Tafuri's historical construction of the Renaissance. It also inevitably shapes Tafuri's reading of the multiple trajectories of the architectural project in relation to the historical project from the Renaissance to the present. And this, too, is why the precarious balance that Alberti struck between the past and the future, like the parallel mediation he effected between the norms and languages of classical antiquity and those of an emerging humanism—relationships characterized more, in the end, by precariousness than by equilibrium—remains an invaluable key to the *progetto storico* of Manfredo Tafuri.

Here it is best to let Tafuri have the last word. When affirming that his method of historical analysis was based on the attempt to describe "forms of contradiction . . . held together 'heroically' . . . by a cultural moment oscillating between the need for certainty and leaps into the unfounded," he observes that this moment has been seen as dialogical. As the discussion proceeds, Tafuri quickly substitutes for this *dialogical* process a *dialectical* one, albeit one of a special kind: a "moment" that remains unresolved, accentuating the energies of striving and incompleteness rather than the achievement of closure and finality: "On the contrary it is possible for history to lend its voice to a dialectical process that does not take the outcome of the struggles it narrates for granted. Hence it must suspend its judgments if it is to proceed at all. Nothing is given as past. Historical time is, by its constitution, hybrid."[147] By adopting this dialectical approach, Tafuri grew with the shifting image of Alberti that unfolded over the years, so that the latter became the object of endless, obsessive study, a sort of "double" who haunted the historian and never left his side. In his critical attempt to reconstitute Alberti and his architectural and cultural universe, the Italian historian invoked not only the ideal aspirations of theory but also the darker anxieties of this complex figure that make both the aspirations and the universe so compelling.

It is in no small measure due to the fact that Tafuri took up the challenge of studying that most fascinating of problems for the student of the Renaissance, the work and the figure of Leon Battista Alberti, that Alberti can be found moving through the background of present-day architecture as a venerable and inspiring shadow, an interlocutor with whom we engage in a dialogue that is perpetually renewed. This dialogue attests to Alberti's centrality in the discipline, registered by the various, often contradictory readings his theory and practice have generated. Among these readings, the one developed by Tafuri stands out for its depth, insight, and originality. To be sure, to locate Tafuri's reflection on Alberti within his larger historical project is one thing; to trace its wider impact on architectural historiography is another. Yet these two tasks are intimately bound together. For it is at least partly because of this project, one that was never content with received wisdom and was always impatient with conventional approaches, that Alberti will undoubtedly reveal new facets of his achievement with the passage of time, fixing us from afar with his unsettling, winged gaze, arrested at mid-flight, at once mobile and at rest, suspended in space between the fleeting and the enduring: the space of architecture.

4 So What? Leon Battista Alberti and the "Invention" of the Architectural Project

Pier Vittorio Aureli

In his book *The Quintessence of Capitalism*, the German sociologist Werner Sombart declared that a fundamental aspect of capitalist subjectivity is the "spirit of undertaking."[1] As Sombart wrote, "undertaking" in its broadest meaning is the realization of a plan "for the carrying out of which is needed . . . the continued co-operation of many individuals under the guidance of a single will."[2] The plan that backs the undertaking must be well-defined and exclude spontaneous or ad hoc initiatives. Unlike the inventor or the genius who is content with their imagination and creative freedom, the "undertaker" must have the capacity to carry a scheme to its realization.[3] Most crucially, they should know that every enterprise is at risk of failing and may be affected by unforeseen circumstances.

The capitalist undertaker invests in speculative initiatives—in what Daniel Defoe would define as the "art of projecting."[4] For Sombart, the diffusion of this entrepreneurial mentality as the art of projecting happened toward the end of the Middle Ages and found one of its most radical developments in the city of Florence. Curiously, Sombart failed to mention that it was in Florence at the beginning of the fifteenth century that the making of buildings shifted from a practice controlled by master builders belonging to the guild system to being the product of a "project" whose plan was devised by a single architect on behalf of patrons. Recent literature on this topic has explained this shift as a gradual process, rather than a sudden revolution—a process in which the architect as a full-fledged designer emerged slowly and not without conflict.[5] Yet it is significant that Sombart dated the emergence of the "spirit of undertaking" to a time in which architecture was increasingly the outcome of predefined projects devised by a recognizable "undertaker": the architect as author. The most celebrated architect practicing in this way was Filippo Brunelleschi who, in the first half of the fifteenth century, realized a series of public monuments for the city of Florence—including the dome of Santa Maria del Fiore—by subordinating the labor of builders to his all-encompassing designs.

However, the figure who provided a theory for the architectural project was not Brunelleschi but Leon Battista Alberti, the author of *De re aedificatoria*, the first Western treatise on architecture written after Vitruvius's *De architectura libri decem*. In *De re aedificatoria*, Alberti insisted on the fact that the architect must devise a careful plan before building begins, and that this plan should not be a vague vision but a precise blueprint of what is going to be realized and how: "I must urge you again and again, before embarking on the work, to weigh up the whole matter on your own and discuss it with experienced advisors. Using scale models, re-examining every part of your proposal two, three, four, seven—up to ten times, taking breaks in between, until from the very roots to the uppermost tile there is nothing, concealed or open, large or small, for which you have not thought out, resolved, and determined, thoroughly and at length, the most handsome and effective position, order and number."[6]

For Alberti, the undertaking of architecture was not based on pure will but on the careful consideration of the available means; indeed, he stated very clearly that no project can be started before any evaluation of its budget. This may sound obvious today, but in Alberti's time the building of monuments evolved over the duration of their construction according to changing public expenditure, so much so that the process regularly had to accommodate shifts in both process and intended outcome. Alberti's idea of the architectural project was also carefully calibrated to the economically efficient realization of a building. Such an understanding of architecture implies a view that is intrinsically defined by economic optimization. Unsurprisingly, in *The Quintessence of Capitalism*, Sombart considered Alberti's writings to be the most important manifestation of the bourgeois spirit of undertaking.[7] However, he was not referring to Alberti the theorist of architecture but to Alberti the author of the influential treatise on household management, *De familia*.[8] Sombart highlighted how *De familia* did not treat household management as an end in itself, that is, as the mere sustenance of a family, but as an apparatus, the goal of which was to increase the economic power of the family as a business enterprise. In doing so, Alberti introduced a well-tempered austerity in which economic power was the product of a logic that quantified every aspect of life.[9] It was precisely this approach—which Sombart defined as quintessentially bourgeois—that became the epistemological framework for Alberti's idea of an architecture driven by *projects* rather than by the empirical experience of master builders.

In the past forty years, the traditional understanding of Alberti as a Renaissance or "universal" man has been replaced by a different portrait: that of a pessimist, ambiguous thinker, and sophisticated manipulator of literary and philosophical sources.[10] In Alberti there is much, much more than petit bourgeois values, yet I would argue that even his "dark side" seems to reinforce his understanding of architectural design as a balancing act; a projective-managerial process in which even the tiniest of details and most uncontrollable of factors must be subsumed within a preconceived plan. Of course, Alberti was not the first to discover that even the most modest form of architecture needs a plan—indeed, a *project*—in order to be built. Karl Marx famously remarked that the difference between the bee and the worst architect is that the former builds its geometrically perfect hive without any preconceived plan, while the second—even when building the most rudimentary structure—needs to first have an idea of the structure itself.[11]

However, if for millennia architects designed and built architecture, it was only from the fifteenth century that architects would design but not necessarily build the architecture themselves. Up until that point, designers who conceived architecture were also master builders, and it was indeed difficult for an individual master builder to be acknowledged as the "author" of a building. Recently, Mario Carpo and Marvin Trachtenberg have reflected on how Alberti's theory of architecture marked a change.[12] By defining the form of a building, the architect also defines the process of its production. The consequence of the preeminence of the project over construction is the complete and rather authoritarian subordination of the workforce that produces architecture to the plan of the architect. Moreover, by linking the work of the architect to the support of a patron, Alberti theorized an architecture that was ultimately subordinated to those who *finance* the act of building. I believe this paradigm shift should be framed as the manifestation of a larger political and economic restructuring of society that happened in Alberti's time: the consolidation of capitalist economy as the main driving force of urban development.

In what follows, I will discuss the political and social implications of Alberti's theory of the architectural *project*. This goes beyond issues of historical scholarship to address the problematic nature of the architectural profession as it evolved in the West. Alberti's interpretation of architecture was far from straightforward, as he lived at a time when the making of buildings was confronted by class conflicts that were impossible to ignore. But it was precisely because of its origins in conflict that the capitalist "spirit of undertaking" demanded architecture to adhere as much as possible to a *project*. The project offered a stable counterpoint both in organizational and rhetorical terms to the volatile conditions in which architecture had to be built. Alberti's theory of the architectural project sat at the very core of this paradoxical situation in which order and disorder, consensus and conflict, harmony and chaos were no longer considered opposing forces but manifestations of the same processes.

Rhetoric and Conflict

It is a telling irony that someone as obsessed with household management as Alberti experienced such a bitter relationship with his relatives, the Alberti family of Florence. Born in the city of Genoa in 1404, Alberti was one of two illegitimate sons of the wealthy merchant Lorenzo di Benedetto Alberti. Lorenzo had been exiled from Florence along with the entire family because they sided with the popular government that came to power during the Ciompi Revolt of 1378. The Alberti family's wealth and popularity among the lower classes had proved a dangerous mixture that prompted their banishment.

Alberti suffered greatly from these vicissitudes, as is made clear in some of his writings.[13] Being the illegitimate son of an exiled father gave him a sense of existential precarity and uprootedness that resulted in two contrasting aspects of his thought: the celebration of the family as the cornerstone of social order and a radical pessimism toward institutions and their capacity to govern society in fairness. It also made him resilient enough to endure difficult circumstances and make the best out of any predicament. Quintessential to this resilience was Alberti's most important intellectual interest, which would influence all his undertakings in both literature and architecture: the art of rhetoric—that is, the art of making things with words.

At an early age, Alberti studied in Padua with Gasparino Barzizza, a prominent grammarian who introduced him to the writings of Cicero. Cicero was a role model for many humanists because he had situated rhetoric—the art of discourse—at the core of intellectual and civic service. Aristotle defined rhetoric as "the faculty of observing in any given case the available means of persuasion."[14] Unlike philosophy, rhetoric is thus a profoundly relational practice because its goal is the persuasion of an audience. It is for this reason that the ultimate place of rhetoric is politics, a sphere where struggle is mediated through words. However, rhetoric can also be an instrument to tame politics since the main goal of the orator is to seek consensus and prevent the eruption of conflict. Cicero lived in one of the most turbulent periods of Roman history, during the final stages of the hundred years of civil war that marked the passage from Republic to Empire. Indeed, he invested himself in rhetoric because he had to confront a situation saturated by conflict; a situation that he believed could be controlled by the power of reason.

It is not by chance that Cicero wrote his major contribution to the art of rhetoric, *De oratore*, at the beginning of the war that finally caused the Republic to implode.[15] Like Cicero, Alberti lived at a time when political instability and social unrest were the norm rather than the exception. The conflict manifested itself with utmost intensity in Florence, and Alberti's family was directly involved in it. At that time, Florence witnessed an unprecedented accumulation of financial capital that was paralleled by an influx of unskilled workers; the textile industry in particular stood at the center of these processes. During the fourteenth century the city was torn apart by several revolts, the last of which was the Ciompi Revolt, led by the wool carders, an underclass barred from forming a guild. This traumatic event highlighted one of the crucial dilemmas of the bourgeois ethos: while the bourgeoisie celebrated the civic liberties of the "people," it also suppressed the liberties of subordinated classes that contested its power.

The Alberti family perfectly embodied this dilemma: having been exiled for supporting the short-lived popular government, they supported the Medici family's rise to power after their banishment from Florence was revoked in 1429. It is in this context of the suppression of social turmoil that the adoption of antiquity as a cultural and ideological model should be situated. Against the possibility of social unrest, humanists such as Coluccio Salutati and Poggio Bracciolini evoked the virtues of an idealized Pax Romana as the blueprint for peaceful civic coexistence.[16] Ciceronian rhetoric was therefore rediscovered as a political technique for the construction of consensus within institutions that were increasingly dominated by powerful elites. His dramatic family circumstances, which had made Alberti wary of politics, led him to focus on family business as the most virtuous (and safe) occupation for the wealthy classes. He was also ambivalent toward institutional power. While *De re aedificatoria* celebrated ethical values as the core of public leadership, emphasizing how good architecture should manifest a sense of justice,[17] Alberti often expressed deep skepticism and disenchantment toward the possibility of fair government. *Momus*, one of his most corrosive texts, penned more or less at the same time as *De re aedificatoria* and *De familia*, is an example.[18] However, this attitude was not exclusive to Alberti, who shared it with other "public intellectuals" of the type that we have, since the nineteenth century, called "humanist."

The Unhappy Consciousness of the Humanists

The humanists were wide-ranging scholars whose main interest was to reconnect their culture to that of the ancients. They were well-versed in Latin (and sometimes Ancient Greek) and focused on reading, translating, and commenting on ancient literature, making it available for contemporary use. The humanists' interest in antiquity was not neutral, as the revival of antiquity was instrumental to rulers and institutions who needed to fabricate an idealized representation of society. They were often sponsored or hired by rulers to write erudite histories of cities that would make the status quo the "natural" consequence of a glorified ancient past.[19] Scholars such as Salutati, Bracciolini, and Leonardo Bruni were not simply men of letters but multitasking cultural advisers who often took prominent political roles as city administrators or occupied managerial positions within the Roman Church. Indeed, a decisive moment for the revival of antiquity happened in Rome in the 1420s under the papacy of Martin V (who ended the Western Schism) when Bracciolini and Bruni began the trend of searching for ancient ruins and inscriptions—an activity that would have a great impact on the young Alberti. The antiquarianism cultivated by prominent figures of the papal office was more than a personal and erudite pursuit; it was also part of a tacit political project aimed toward a *translatio imperii*, the translation of the ideological charisma of the Roman Empire into the political leadership of the Church. This cultural appropriation of Roman antiquity became a model that many rulers soon copied.

As the democratic ethos of the *comuni* was replaced by the oligarchic and autocratic rule of *signoria* (lordship), the role of humanists as cultural counselors became increasingly necessary, as they offered ideological legitimacy by masking the opaque politics of governments with the prestige of antiquity. Yet the humanists were not passive facilitators of power. Paradoxically, their reputation was based on their role as independent scholars driven by a pursuit of knowledge, fame, and civic respectability. Humanists did not belong to a guild or corporation, and their individual authorship was their most important capital. Even if their knowledge—like any form of knowledge—was the product of exchange and sharing, they had to cultivate a reputation as clearly recognizable "authors."[20] This was the source of Alberti's obsession with the idea of the author—and, by extension, of the architect-as-author—as the embodiment of *authority*. Indeed, as Trachtenberg has emphasized, the author was not only considered a creator in humanist culture but also the validator of both the form and meaning of a literary work.[21] In this sense, the *auctor* is the person who has *auctoritas* over a text or any other artifact, and it was such literary and artistic authority that fifteenth-century institutions of power tried to appropriate as a fundamentally ideological weapon.

Italian humanists were what today we would call *cultural entrepreneurs*: freelance intellectual workers whose main goal was the cultivation of their own "authorial capital." In spite of their social prestige, humanists lived a precarious existence, and this condition made them ideologically flexible. They were not above using ancient texts in an opportunistic fashion, collaging different sources to create content that would be useful to specific purposes—a method that would become prominent in Alberti's approach to architecture. Rejecting the systematic character of scholastic thought, the humanists engineered a form of cultural production that was both independent and subservient, secular and deeply poisoned by power interests. The ambivalence of such a position was reflected in their eagerness to serve power in any of its forms and in their disenchantment and cynicism toward that same power—a sentiment that often surfaced in their literary production.[22] As such, the humanists embodied an unresolvable conflict between intellectual autonomy and dependence on power: the "unhappy consciousness" of the bourgeoisie. Alberti's intellectual ideals were deeply influenced by this ambivalence, and it is exactly this subjectivity that animated his role as an intellectual and his understanding of the architectural project.

Alberti's Ambiguities

The scholar who best highlighted Alberti's ambivalence toward institutions of power was perhaps Eugenio Garin. While in his early writings on Alberti he emphasized Alberti's philosophical progressivism, Garin penned two essays in the 1970s in which he attacked the myth of Alberti as a "universal man" focused on metaphysical harmony.[23] Against such interpretations, Garin highlighted Alberti's skepticism about society, a view supported by his reevaluation of two rather disconcerting literary works: the *Intercoenales* and *Momus*. Written in the form of dialogues to be read during dinner, the *Intercoenales* (*Dinner Pieces*) are short narrative meditations on human life. These stories are bizarre and at times nightmarish vignettes that Garin compared to Hieronymus Bosch's painted visions of monstrous figures. One deals with a voyage on the moon; another with the story of a man who, given the chance to witness his own funeral, realizes with great despair that his most precious possession—his library—has been dispersed, and that his relatives are happy to be rid of him.[24] As Alberti himself revealed, the central theme of the *Intercoenales* is the relationship between virtue and fortune. In Alberti's view, no matter how virtuous one is, fortune or *chance* always wins; the text thus presents the world as an improbable phantasmagoria of deceptive images in which any aspiration to truth and justice is frustrated by mockery, confusion, and disillusionment with humanity's potential to overcome these evils. For Alberti, the only possibility to coexist with this hopeless reality is through *patientia* (patience)—stoic endurance.

This rather somber outlook was even more explicit in Alberti's satirical novel *Momus*. Its eponymous antihero is a rather dodgy minor deity that Alberti describes as "an aggressive obstructionist, hostile and annoying,"[25] who is banned from Heaven after criticizing none other than Jupiter. Momus's contempt for Jupiter is motivated by the fact that the latter has created mortals whose ambitions have a negative impact on the gods themselves. Exiled on Earth, he undermines the gods by persuading mortals that prayer is useless while also trying to convince women to make votive offerings in order to enhance their beauty. Momus is eventually accepted into Heaven and pretends to be a loyal member of Jupiter's court in order to stay there. In his new role, he writes a philosophical text to guide Jupiter in making the world a better place. Jupiter ignores Momus's advice and gives up this ambition because he realizes mortals already worship the gods anyway. Having scrapped his plans, Jupiter reads Momus's notes and regrets not following his advice, while poor Momus is castrated and tied to a rock by Juno in punishment for his misogyny. In spite of its surreal quality, the novel is full of subliminal messages that qualify this bizarre story as a cautionary tale about the misery of power and the stupidity of the institutions that Alberti himself served. Some aspects can be read as autobiographical references; apart from the obvious theme of exile, Jupiter's refusal to listen to Momus seems to echo Alberti's relationship with Nicholas V, the pope who wanted to rebuild Rome as the true successor of ancient Rome.[26] *Momus* described the denizens of Heaven—or perhaps the Vatican Curia—in all their weakness, hypocrisy, and chronic volubility.

Unsurprisingly, the character Momus praises the vagrant who has no master to serve but the self. Because their existence is worthless in the eyes of society, vagabonds are free to speak the truth and thus can abandon themselves to radical *parrhesia*, or candid speech. Reading such an appraisal, one cannot avoid being shocked by the fact that it was written by the author of *De familia*, in which Alberti insisted on the importance of the household as the core of society. Garin suggested that *Momus*, *De familia*, and *De re aedificatoria* should be read in parallel,[27] as Alberti's dialogic method implied that he did not fully identify with any of the views he voiced. If his reflections on the family and on architecture demonstrated his "projective" and institutional approach, Alberti offered rather more destructive commentaries on society and life itself in *Momus*, the *Intercoenales*, and other writings.

Manfredo Tafuri, in his important essay on Alberti and Pope Nicholas V,[28] followed Garin's interpretation and argued that *Momus* might have expressed Alberti's critical stance toward the pope and his ambition to redesign Rome as a majestic representation of the Church's spiritual and political role. Tafuri's interpretation countered the opinion of many authors who believed that Alberti had to have been the main counselor of the pope's plan; indeed, Matteo Palmieri's famous chronicle of that project included an anecdote in which Alberti presented *De re aedificatoria* to Nicholas V. However, Tafuri noted that this episode appeared only after Palmieri explained how Alberti had advised the pope not to proceed with the centerpiece of his *renovatio urbis*, the rebuilding of Saint Peter's, and suggested instead the restoration of the existing basilica. In this light, it is possible to read Alberti's presentation of *De re aedificatoria* not as a way to legitimize the pope's plan but as an attempt to reinforce Alberti's authority as *architect*.[29] Remarkably, this anecdote sees the architect advise the patron *not* to undertake building activity, and thus marks the birth of the architect-as-intellectual-worker; as someone who can choose not to build, or better, who has sufficient authority to oppose building. There is something Melvillean in this stance, which "prefers not to," rather than viewing architecture as the mere execution of the patron's order.[30] For Tafuri, this confirmed Alberti's critical position toward institutions of power such as the Church.

However, Alberti's position might not have been as radical as Tafuri thought. Consider the fact that Alberti's idea of the architectural project ultimately solidified the relationship between patron and architect at the expense of the figure who, until that moment, had been the indisputable protagonist of architecture: the master builder. Strangely, Garin and Tafuri, both so concerned with Alberti's attitudes toward power, remained silent on the nature of his attempt to reframe architectural design as a plan to which buildings—and builders—were strictly subordinated.

Alberti's theory and his projects, I believe, are not the dialectical counterpart of his rather destructive commentary on society but rather the logical conclusion of such "negative" thinking. There is a profound solidarity between the "dark" and "bright" sides of Alberti's writings, as if his critical commentary on society served as the starting point for an idea of architecture that would respond to its negative context by digesting rather than negating it. The architectural project as plan thus appeared to constitute a possibility for architecture to both coexist with and resist the precariousness of its increasingly unstable social context.

In Alberti's thought, architecture is suspended between the calculating and managerial reason expressed in his *De familia*, the humanist approach to rhetorical persuasion, and a sense of skepticism about the possibility of an enduring state of order and harmony. The architectural project he theorized was thus situated within a delicate balance of certainty and uncertainty, order and disorder, harmony and disruption, faith and distrust in institutions, celebration of building craft and subordination of builders, idealism and pessimism. These dichotomies become fully visible when one revisits *De re aedificatoria* and some of the buildings that have been attributed to Alberti.

Lineaments

How did Alberti become interested in the "art of building"? It is not so obvious that a humanist so at ease with ancient literature and rhetoric should focus on such a craft-driven activity as building—building and *not* architecture. *De re aedificatoria*—aptly titled to distinguish it from Vitruvius's *De architectura*—contains very few mentions of the word *architecture*. While the book also discusses large-scale undertakings such as the making of streets and other citywide proposals, it is the singular building as a clearly defined artifact that interests Alberti. This is perhaps the most outstanding difference between *De re aedificatoria* and *De architectura*.[31] Conceived as an encyclopedia, Vitruvius's *De architectura* includes many topics that exceed what, even today, would be associated with the discipline of architecture, from the making of cities to sundials and war machines. For Vitruvius, architecture represented the possibility of planning the totality of the built environment, an all-encompassing form of knowledge: the *arkhé*—the first principle—of potentially *everything*. In *De architectura*, the technical aspects of design are prominent precisely because Vitruvius focused on architecture as a multiscalar activity, the goal of which is the reduction of the entire physical world to a well-functioning machine.

As is well known, Alberti criticized Vitruvius's lack of clarity in *De architectura*,[32] maintaining that it was so obscure as to not matter at all. It is obvious that Alberti's ambition was to replace Vitruvius's ten books with his own ten books—a round figure that symbolized completeness and perfection both in Western antiquity and in the Renaissance. Fragments of *De architectura* had been known since medieval times, but it was Alberti's friend and colleague Poggio Bracciolini who had rediscovered and made the manuscript known in its entirety. Humanists were impressed by Vitruvius's *De architectura* not only because it was the only extant architecture treatise dating to classical antiquity, but also because of its systematic approach, which suggested that everything that exists as a material artifact can ultimately be rationally planned. The humanists knew that Vitruvius wrote *De architectura* with an ideal audience (and patron) in mind: the first Roman emperor, Augustus, to whom the book is dedicated. Augustus rose to power and became the first de facto emperor after a long civil war—a predicament addressed by Vitruvius in his dedication. *De architectura* and *De re aedificatoria* resonated with the humanist invocation of Pax Romana against the threat of political turmoil; both the Roman civil wars and the social conflicts of the late fourteenth century were rooted in social inequality, and they both challenged the facade of republican ethos that animated both ancient Rome and powerful medieval *comuni* such as Florence. Against a backdrop of class conflict, the appeal to social order and civic responsibility became a way to naturalize social inequality while framing any form of antagonism as irrational and counterproductive.

Vitruvius and his Renaissance readers imagined architecture as an apparatus, the main goal of which was to reinforce a sense of civic stability against the fragmentation brought about by social unrest. But while in Vitruvius there is a balance between the technical and the rhetorical dimension of architecture, in Alberti the rhetorical dimension is more prominent. It is not by chance that

Alberti's conception of beauty was no longer the metaphysical and abstract *venustas* invoked by Vitruvius, but the more relational and practical *concinnitas*, a term borrowed from Cicero, who used it to address the efficacy of a rhetorical composition.

An important aspect of Vitruvius's theory of architecture was his distinction between *fabrica* and *ratiocinatio*.[33] While *fabrica* referred to the practice of building, *ratiocinatio* referred to reasoning, or the conception of the building before the building itself began: the *project*. This distinction implied a strict dependency of building on reasoning, as there is no *fabrica* without *ratiocinatio*, and the latter was what legitimized the role of the architect. Vitruvius's distinction became a powerful precedent for the invention of the architectural project in the fifteenth century, as it already hypostatized design as something separate from construction, an idea that had been virtually unthinkable in medieval Europe. This distinction mirrors one of the fundamental principles of the capitalist division of labor: the separation of manual and intellectual labor, and the hegemony of the latter over the former.[34]

Alberti's construction of the primacy of reasoning over the practice of building took a far more radical stance than Vitruvius's. As Carpo has emphasized, Alberti did not view the architect as a master builder but as an *author* who provided a plan for a building in the form of *notations* (drawings and models) to be followed as faithfully as possible by those who *build* architecture.[35] In *De re aedificatoria*, Alberti laments the tendency to change plans while a building was already under construction—this was a routine occurrence on medieval building sites—depending on necessity or the initiative of the master builder.[36] Under such circumstances, project and building craft were one and the same. Trachtenberg defines this condition as "building-in-time": a process in which construction was not rigidly controlled by a plan but unfolded organically according to contingencies.[37] As examples, Trachtenberg cites medieval monuments such as cathedrals, the construction of which often spanned across generations and the plans for which were constantly adjusted.

This mode of production empowered the master builder and made construction irreducible to an all-encompassing design for which every detail was defined in advance. For Trachtenberg, Alberti's theory was meant to counter this understanding of architecture as building-in-time with an idea of architecture that suppressed any temporal dimension: everything that was to be built would be decided in advance. As Carpo has suggested, Alberti understood the building as a mechanical imprint of the notations provided by the architect themself. It would take centuries before such a reorganization of architectural production would be fully implemented, but Alberti's theory already implied a completely new understanding of building, both in terms of execution and of form.

The first book of *De re aedificatoria* is dedicated to what Alberti defined as *lineamenta*, or the "lineaments." By "lineaments," Alberti meant an abstraction of the building's geometry into lines. In order to *project* architecture, the architect must reduce the building to its main lines: "All the intent and purpose of lineaments lies in finding the correct, *infallible* way of joining and fitting together those lines and angles which define and enclose the surface of the building."[38] The lineaments must set out the order of the building: its position, scale, exact proportions, and the composition of its parts so that the entire form of the building "may depend on the lineaments alone."[39] For Alberti, they had no immanent relationship with the material reality of the building. Rather, the drawing of architecture as an abstract composition of lines and angles was "conceived in the mind . . . and perfected in the learned intellect and imagination" of the architect.[40] This is perhaps one of the most influential conceptualizations of architecture as *project*. "To project" means, literally, to put or throw something forward. Within the realm of geometry, "project" can also be interpreted as *projection*, an operation which allows the translation of points and lines from one plane to another. It is interesting to note that Alberti recommended the rigorous use of orthogonal projection for drawing plans, sections, and elevations while he discouraged the use of more pictorial techniques of representation. In his view, exceedingly detailed and complex models were unnecessary and even deceptive. Instead, he recommended simplifying models as their purpose was, essentially, to show the lineaments. Ultimately, Alberti's theory implied that the project was a fundamental *abstraction* of architectural form.

There is no doubt that the source of this method was Alberti's role model, Filippo Brunelleschi, to whom he so emphatically dedicated his first foray in the arts: *De pictura*. Born in Florence a generation before Alberti, Brunelleschi was a goldsmith and sculptor who only became involved in architecture later in life. Apart from its innovative form, which was inspired by a direct knowledge of ancient Roman architecture, Brunelleschi's built work was also groundbreaking in how it approached the building site. As his biographer, Antonio di Tuccio Manetti, has shown, Brunelleschi expected master builders to faithfully execute his plan. This approach is clearly reflected in the form of his architecture, which is strictly geometrical and organized through a defined syntactical order. In buildings such as the 1420s loggia of the Ospedale degli Innocenti, all of the columns and ornamental features obey a unitary design and seem to manifest the overall diagram of the building's generative process. In Brunelleschi's buildings, lineaments are not just the diagram of the architecture, but the architecture itself. His architecture embodied the fact that it was an outcome of *disegno*, a concept that would emerge later in artistic discourse but found one of its first written formulations in Alberti's theory of lineaments.[41]

Disegno, the reduction of architecture to its lineaments, ultimately empowered architects and disenfranchised builders. Such a shift was met with unrepressed hostility from master builders.[42] Antiquarian erudition became the prerogative of the architect: classical features such as columns, frames, and standardized ornamental details, "correctly" used, were tools with which the architect countered the initiative of individual stonecutters, controlling the process of building and making the building itself a pure index of the architect's design. On the construction site of the dome of Santa Maria del Fiore, Brunelleschi famously refused to disclose the entirety of his plans to the builders, so that his role would become indispensable. According to Carpo, such an attitude singled out the role of the architect as the "author" whose plan could not be changed by the builders.[43]

Yet we should not forget that the authority of the architect ultimately depended—and depends—on the patron. By empowering the architect as author, the patron granted themself more direct control of the building. After all, it was the patron and not the architect who *decided* on the architectural project by financing its construction. It was not a coincidence that wealthy patrons were the intended audience of Alberti's *De re aedificatoria*—a treatise written in Latin, which very few craftsmen could understand. The book was not a manual for the architect, who at the time was still a builder and therefore unlikely to be sympathetic to Alberti's position. Instead, it encouraged patrons to empower the figure of the architect in ways that would become increasingly common in the centuries that followed. For Alberti, the role of the patron was decisive and therefore they had to be architecturally literate, in terms of both cultural and technical issues. Thus, his idea of the architectural project did not reinforce the autonomous role of the architect as much as it did the power of the client.

Within this framework, the project became the enterprise described by Sombart, whose undertaker was neither the builder nor the architect but whosoever had the financial means to invest in it. Understood in this way, the project does not only define the form of the building but also the execution of it, ensuring that its every aspect is predefined according to measurable parameters. The reliance on measure, geometry, and proportions advocated by Alberti played a great role in the development of Renaissance architecture, but perhaps not in the metaphysical way celebrated by historians such as Rudolf Wittkower and Erwin Panofsky.[44] After Alberti, architecture would increasingly be produced through the exactitude of numbers, an attitude of quantification that mirrored, in design, the pervasive role that money and financial surplus would come to have in the organization of social life in the early modern West.[45] Unlike the elastic temporality of premodern architecture, the modern project as conceived by Alberti presupposed an abstract temporality that was *measurable* and thus compatible with financial parameters.

This condition was evident in the way Alberti understood the role of architectural representation. Early Italian practitioners of architectural design, such as Giotto or Brunelleschi, were usually trained as painters or sculptors. Although Alberti acknowledged the importance of painting skills in the practice of architectural design, in his *De re aedificatoria* he was adamant that architectural drawing was to be considered autonomous from the art of painting.[46] Unlike painting, the purpose of which, for Alberti, was the representation of reality as we *see* it, the architectural drawing was a form of notation that was not meant to encode or communicate a subjective perception of space, but rather its *measure*. The same approach extended to three-dimensional models, which Alberti highlighted the usefulness of in allowing architects and patrons to test design solutions, but also as tools to calculate expenses, making architecture mathematically quantifiable.

It is interesting to note that such an understanding of models as spatial schemes was very similar to the compositional logic of Brunelleschi's architecture, in which the organizing geometry was clearly rendered through features such as columns, entablatures, and arches, which made tangible the diagram that governed them. In both Brunelleschi's practice and Alberti's theory of architecture, the geometric abstraction of architecture—that is to say, the process through which architecture was made *quantifiable*—became the form of architecture itself. Architectural drawing as *disegno* or "design" was therefore connected to the rise both of the architect as intellectual practitioner and of the monetary economy—a realm in which measuring everything was a fundamental precondition for the creation and exchange value of things.

Ornament and Structure

For Alberti, the abstraction implied in the design process was counterbalanced by the emphasis given to ornament as a core feature of architecture. These seemingly opposite concepts were in fact complementary, as they defined the two poles of the architectural undertaking: the calculation of reason and rhetorical impetus.

On the one hand, the building was governed by a design made of abstract lineaments, and on the other, it was manifested as a recognizable architecture only through its ornamentation. Alberti's theory was dominated by this dichotomy, which was accentuated by the fact that *De re aedificatoria* was conceived as two rather distinct parts. While Books 1 to 5 defined architecture in terms of design, technique, and building functions, Books 6 to 10 tackled architecture as ornament. In the first part, Alberti focused on materials, construction, "public works" (such as town planning, city walls, bridges, the sewage system, streets, and squares), and "private works" (such as palaces, castles, villas, housing, monasteries, military camps, jails, and temples). In this part of the treatise, Alberti was careful to make his remarks as general as possible, as if to demonstrate that his theory of architecture was not biased by his personal idiosyncrasies but rather founded on principles that were supposedly universal. Things become more complicated from Book 6 onward. After the completion of the first five books, Alberti appeared to be exhausted and explicitly and unconventionally expressed as much at the beginning of the text. Indeed, in the rest of *De re aedificatoria*, he essentially revisited topics he had already tackled in the previous books, returning—again—to public and private buildings, this time centering not on the abstract conception of architecture through lineaments but on its visible manifestation through ornament.

It is possible to argue that for Alberti, ornament *was* architecture itself. If lineaments represented a design tool, ornament was what gave a *form* to building. In order to understand this shift, it is useful to go back to Brunelleschi and understand the shortcomings of his syntactical method. At first glance, Brunelleschi's architecture seems to be governed by a logic in which ornamental and tectonic features more or less coincide. For example, in monumental structures such as the Ospedale and the churches of Santo Spirito and San Lorenzo, arches were structural features supported by load-bearing columns. Yet Brunelleschi was often unable to carry out this logic in all aspects of his buildings. Often, he ended up in situations where what ought to have been structural elements were instead merely ornamental, such as in the monumental entablature that marks the walls of the Old Sacristy in San Lorenzo. When materialized, Brunelleschi's *disegno* was ambiguous and thus unable to maintain its radical purity of structural form. In his theory, Alberti solved this conundrum by making architectural form an ornament whose goal was to "dress" the bare structure of the building. While lineaments defined the overall logic of the architectural organism, architecture-as-ornament gave to this organism an intelligible, pleasing image. Contrary to Brunelleschi's failed attempt to use the logic of classical architecture as a basis for tectonic design, Alberti's use of the orders was completely independent of the structure of the building. This approach destabilized or even challenged the conception of architecture he introduced in Book 1 with the theory of lineaments.

Following the Vitruvian triad of *firmitas*, *utilitas*, and *venustas*, Alberti focused on the first two in Books 1 to 5 of *De re aedificatoria*. From Books 6 to 9, the main theme was *venustas*. Yet while for Vitruvius *venustas* was a metaphysical attribute of architecture, a sort of ideal of perfection that transcended the specificity of each building, for Alberti it was a much more relational condition. He defined beauty as "harmony between parts according to reason": when something is beautiful nothing can be changed, added, or subtracted. Alberti recognized that such an idea of beauty was unattainable—even in "nature" itself. Thus, in order to manifest itself, beauty needed something less perfect but more concrete: something that he identified as ornament. For Alberti, ornament was a sort of "auxiliary light" through which something beautiful could be made visible; he seems to suggest that without the more pedestrian and relative fact of ornament, beauty would be unattainable. A potential side effect of this theory of ornament is that it ultimately relativizes beauty: if something as relative as ornament is the only possible way for architecture to render beauty visible, then beauty becomes an attribute open to interpretation. Against this possibility, Alberti invoked the prescriptive and normative role of theory: ornament can only work if it follows a "consistent method and art."[47]

In order to define this method, for the first time in the history of Western architecture Alberti tried to reconstruct the origins of architecture, thus instrumentalizing architectural history as a way to justify a design theory. Interestingly, however, he refused to flatten the mythical origins of architecture into an absolute canon because, as he explained, "The arts were born of adversity and observation, fostered by use and experiment, and matured by knowledge and reason."[48] Note how at the beginning of everything Alberti placed the very contingent, hostile, and empirical conditions of adversity and observation; he then followed them up with use and trial and error, which cannot be reduced to the certainty of a formula. Only at end of the historical process did he position knowledge and reason. The "consistent method of the arts" was thus rooted in a process that was deeply antitheoretical and antimetaphysical, which Alberti exposed in all its fragility and volatility. It is for this reason that the metaphysical *venustas* was not at the core of Alberti's theory of architecture; instead, it was the more performative and pragmatic *concinnitas*.

This concept was a readaptation of a trope elaborated by Cicero in his two major contributions to the art of rhetoric, *De oratore* and *De officiis*. For Cicero, *concinnitas* was the ability to achieve an elegant *congruity between parts* according to principles summarized in three categories: *numerus* ("number" or measure), *finitio* ("finiteness"), and *collocatio* ("collocation"). According to Alberti, number defined the building as a body made of parts, whose organization obeyed mathematical proportions; finiteness could be understood as the *outline* of things; and collocation was the positioning of architectural elements in their proper place. It is important to note that there was nothing absolute about these principles, as everything depended on the situation with which they interacted. As the ultimate referent for the appreciation of the *concinnitas* of objects, Alberti mentioned *ratio innata*, the faculty of judgment through which the human mind structures its experience of reality. This means that the capacity to judge whether something is beautiful was not hypostatized according to some divine canon but was construed as innately human.

According to Alberti, it is the subject, who experiences architecture under specific conditions, who decides whether something is beautiful or not. Like the art of rhetoric, in which the orator must confront a specific situation and thus adapt their speech to it, the architect must define the *concinnitas* of architecture by constructing a plausible order of things, the goal of which is to please and persuade an audience; *use* and *experience* were the fundamental sources of *concinnitas*. For this reason, it could only be manifested through ornament, because unlike beauty itself—which was understood as an unchanging paradigm—ornament was concretely rooted in the specific culture that produced it. Hidden behind the rhetoric of *concinnitas* lurked an idea of architectural "perfection" that was radically contingent, nonabsolute, and thus uncertain. The uncertainty at the heart of *concinnitas* was even more radical if we consider Alberti's skepticism of the human faculty of judgement. After all, while writing *De re aedificatoria*, he was also writing *Momus*—a story that portrayed both humans and gods as completely devoid of any *ratio innata*.

For Alberti, however, the actual objective of *concinnitas* was, rather pragmatically, consensus—and ultimately the taming of conflicts. This aim was made clear in a remarkable passage: "What other human art might sufficiently protect a building and save it from human attack? Beauty may even influence an enemy, by restraining his anger and so preventing the work being violated. Thus I might be so bold as to state: No other means is as effective in protecting a work from damage and human injury as is dignity and grace of form."[49]

Here the necessity of ornament and *concinnitas* vis-à-vis conflict and violence was made explicit. Five hundred years before Le Corbusier, Alberti spelled out the motto of (bourgeois) architecture: *Architecture or revolution?* Alberti's passage bespeaks an unprecedented realism because its unusual reference to violence—which Vitruvius reserved only for the military aspects of his theory—clearly referred to the unstable times in which he was living and practicing. It was precisely in this condition that the link between architecture and rhetoric became useful, as the art of rhetoric addressed a precarious situation in which the dialectic between conflict and persuasion, order and disorder, could always go off-balance and disrupt civic order.

Like other humanists, Alberti developed a keen interest in the *history* of architecture. Much as antiquarians would "reconstruct" the history of cities or kingdoms in order to legitimize their existence, the architect would refer to this history in order to prove the certainty of their architectural principles. As Alberti rooted *concinnitas* in experience and use, he could only justify it through historical genealogy. It was no coincidence that, after discussing this concept, he provided one of the first Western attempts to present what we can call a history of architecture. Alberti's history put in sequence places and periods—from the Egyptians to the Greeks, the Etruscan to the Romans—in order to posit ancient Roman architecture as the logical conclusion of this genealogy. This is perhaps the origin of architects' long-standing love affair with the history of their discipline. Only by referring to the (idealized) past in the form of precedents could the architect establish a sense of legitimacy. As demonstrated by the history of political institutions, there is no authority without (its own) history.

Alberti theorized not only the project as a design that preceded and dictated construction, but also the possibility of architecture legitimizing its own authority through the instrumentalization of history. What are Alberti's designs for the Tempio Malatestiano in Rimini or Palazzo Rucellai in Florence if not extremely sophisticated essays on history, written for patrons in search of (historical) legitimacy? Yet he was not entirely at ease with historicism. His literary writings are peppered with consternation regarding the hypocrisy of intellectual fabrications that referenced ancient authors. One of the most telling examples of this attitude is the poem that he dedicated to the fly, celebrating the most annoying and useless of insects as the most perfect being on Earth, just to mock the power of rhetoric to manipulate anything at will.[50] For Alberti, history did the same: even the most improbable situations could acquire a respectable pedigree.

The Tempio Malatestiano, Rimini

The relationship between Alberti's theory and the small number of projects attributed to him has been the subject of much discussion, but there is a general consensus that it is difficult to trace a direct link between theory and practice in his work. According to recent scholarship on the buildings attributed to him, it is uncertain to what extent he was involved in their design, as he often worked through an intermediary architect to whom he would send written instructions and perhaps drawings and models.[51] Even if Alberti emphasized the authorial role of the architect, he also recommended that they collaborate with experts who would eventually share the blame in case things did not go as planned.

The most famous of Alberti's letters to his collaborators is the one sent to Matteo de' Pasti, the on-site architect at the Tempio Malatestiano (Malatesta Temple) in Rimini. In this letter, he sent precise instructions and a small drawing—inserted in the text itself—to illustrate the motif that should link the upper and lower part of the facade. In a crucial passage, Alberti commented on criticisms leveled at his design choices by a local builder, probably reported to him by de' Pasti himself. These criticisms were perhaps an understandable reaction to his radical design proposals, such as the ambition to top the building with a gigantic dome. Alberti replied that his design choices should not be questioned as he referenced ancient and prestigious monuments such as the Pantheon. Such an argument would silence any opposition, given that the Tempio Malatestiano was meant to celebrate the clan of the notorious warlord Sigismondo Malatesta, whose ambition was to make Rimini the Rome of his kingdom. To give a tangible sign of this grand vision, Sigismondo wanted to transform a fourteenth-century Franciscan church into his family mausoleum, as the Malatesta Temple.

Alberti provided a design that was a compendium not just of references to ancient Roman architecture but also of his own design method. With the exception of the vaulting of the main nave, the enlargement of the choir, and the building of the gigantic dome, the project for the Tempio was essentially the project of a facade enclosing the exterior walls of the existing church. This choice highlighted two important principles theorized by Alberti: the role of the wall as the main datum of architecture, and the use of classical orders as applied ornament. According to Alberti, columns should always support entablatures, not arches. Both columns and entablatures were considered ornamental features to be applied to walls, like a dress covering a body, while arches were viewed as structural elements—essentially as openings in a wall—that could be framed by decorative classical columns but not supported by them. This understanding of the architectural orders vis-à-vis the structural nature of the wall offered the Albertian design method great flexibility, yet it also undermined the value of classical orders as tectonic elements. For example, in the Tempio Malatestiano the orders clearly define the *disegno* of the
fig. 4.1 lower facade: four columns support an imposing entablature. However, the continuity of the entablature is broken by forward-projecting elements in correspondence with the columns, almost suggesting that this composition has no tectonic value. Moreover, the same entablature wraps around the side of the building as if floating, this time without its "supporting" columns. Instead, the side facades are defined by a sequence of arches piercing an austere wall, the ornamental minimalism of which contrasts the wealth of ornamental features on the main facade.

While the facade recalls a triumphal arch, echoing the nearby Arch of Augustus, the sides may refer to ancient aqueducts. If we add the projected dome—which was never built—to this composition, the result is an unprecedented collage of ancient architectural tropes that aimed to make the building a distillate of recognizable Roman features. Rhetorically, the composition imposed on the existing church—and by extension, on the city

4.1 Alberti, Tempio Malatestiano, Rimini, Italy. Photo: Davide Piras / Alamy Stock Photo.

around it—the convention of (new) classical orders as something that was meant to correct the existing context by using the power of a "Roman," and thus indisputable, language. In this sense, one of the most astonishing features of the Tempio Malatestiano is the misalignment between the arches of the new side facades
fig. 4.2 and the existing windows of the Gothic church. The new arches frame the old windows, allowing light into the vast interior, and yet they follow a different rhythm; with great pragmatism, Alberti decided not to hide this misalignment but to exhibit it, as if the new structure exemplified the "editorial" power of ancient Roman architecture over the more "barbaric" medieval structure.

Unlike in Brunelleschi's design approach, which saw the edifice unfold into a three-dimensional structural system, Alberti's architecture can be considered compositions of facades that were each capable of becoming an autonomous entity. This approach to the building seems to undermine Alberti's conception of architecture as a coherent whole. And yet his understanding of beauty as *concinnitas*, the possibility of keeping together irreducible parts in a coherent whole, was perfectly congruent with his actual design method. After all, his idea of architecture as a coherent whole acquired much more value when it was capable of accepting—and turning to its own advantage—the inevitable imperfection of mundane reality. Indeed, only at first glance do his facades appear to be very strict compositions; upon closer examination, they reveal all their slippery nature, as if Alberti was deliberately undermining the possibility of achieving perfect coherence among the different parts of the building. Rather than aspiring to absolute coherence, as Brunelleschi did with his own syntactical language, Alberti not only accepted imperfection but used it as a method of design; as a way of making architecture adaptable to even the most difficult situation. A radical example of this method is his most famous facade: Palazzo Rucellai in Florence, executed from 1446 to 1451.

Palazzo Rucellai, Florence

fig. 4.3 Alberti's design for Palazzo Rucellai consists of a facade applied to existing buildings—a group of properties that the patron Giovanni di Paolo Rucellai wanted to unite as one family complex.

4.2 Alberti, Tempio Malatestiano, Rimini, Italy. Photo: Raphael Salzedo / Alamy Stock Photo.

4.3 Alberti, Palazzo Rucellai, Florence, Italy. Photo: Album / Alamy Stock Photo.

The facade is striking in its flatness, and even more remarkable when we consider that the design derives from the overlapping of two ornamental features that usually work three-dimensionally: *bugnato* ("rusticated masonry") and, for the first time in domestic architecture, the superimposition of classical orders.

In order to understand the rhetorical power of these features, it is worth considering another Florentine palazzo built just before Rucellai's: Palazzo Medici, designed by Michelozzo di Bartolomeo and executed between 1444 and 1484. This building established the canon of the Renaissance patrician *palazzo* with a quadrangular form, facades defined by even fenestration, a courtyard framed by loggias, and an enclosed garden. An entire district was demolished to accommodate the building; its construction along one of the most important streets of Florence, the Via Larga, was intended as a way to consolidate the family's influence in local politics. When approached from the cathedral, Palazzo Medici would have appeared as an imposing block standing against the informality of the medieval urban fabric. The exterior of the building is monumentalized by a richly decorated entablature edging its roof and massive *bugnato* rustication that gradually flattens toward its top. The facade, which is pierced by evenly distributed windows, was meant to reference that of Palazzo della Signoria, the town hall built in the mid-fourteenth century at the height of Florentine republican sentiment. The Medici's architectural appropriation of this key place of civic power was meant to highlight their new role as officious *signoria* of Florence. As such, Palazzo Medici became the model of subsequent *palazzi* in Florence, including Palazzo Rucellai, although this building responded to the archetype with substantial twists.

Palazzo Rucellai follows Palazzo Medici's emulation of the medieval town hall in its use of rustication and arched windows with central columns, thus celebrating the patron's alliance with the powerful Medici. Yet in Palazzo Rucellai, the rustication is framed by a grid formed by columns and entablatures, suggesting a more "civilized" version of the ubiquitous medieval urban fortresses that represented the military power of wealthy clans. As mentioned, the main goal of the building's facade was to give a coherent interface to the properties acquired by the Rucellai through time; to achieve this task, the design exploited the clear geometry and solemn grandeur of classical orders, hinting at Roman monuments such as the Colosseum and the Septizonium. The main facade was explicitly designed as an incomplete architecture, as if to suggest that the palazzo could eventually be expanded, and the regularity of its composition aimed at the establishment of a flexible system rather than the imposition of an absolute form. For this reason, Palazzo Rucellai looks more discreet than Palazzo Medici and more "bourgeois" in the literal sense of the word: more urbane and less inclined to celebrate in bombastic terms the power of a clan, perhaps revealing Alberti's disenchantment with the discord of Renaissance politics.

While Palazzo Medici confronted the city antagonistically by dint of its scale and the aggressive character of its form, Palazzo Rucellai appeared eager to be part of the city. The superposed classical orders are decisive in shaping this impression, as they had never been used for a private building until Alberti introduced them; they did not feature at Palazzo Medici. In Palazzo Rucellai, they are an ornamental feature that imposes a regular rhythm on the preexisting structures. Coordinating construction with such a determined classical *disegno* was not an easy task, as premodern buildings—especially residential ones—were far from geometrically regular. In the conflictual yet fluid medieval city, structures would grow incrementally, claiming and negotiating every space available. The distribution of openings—doors and windows, loggias, balconies—would result in ad hoc compositions that were difficult to regularize.

Only in the fourteenth century could powerful *comuni* such as Siena and Florence impose regulations that demanded a more coherent relationship between private buildings and their urban context. During this period, the facades of private buildings began to be understood as public artifacts, and a regular distribution of openings became a signifier of publicness, especially for the wealthier urban merchant and artisan classes. However, when the social mobility of the late Middle Ages came to an end in the early fifteenth century and elites started to both solidify and take over the democratic structures of power, the facade became an ambivalent semantic image. On the one hand, this image invoked stability and the necessity of a public order, while on the other, it expressed the prestige of families whose influence over the politics of republican cities such as Florence was becoming increasingly problematic. Alberti's use of the orders seemed to act as mediator in this conflict. In correcting and taming Palazzo Medici's aggressive appropriation of the architecture of the town hall, his design opted for a more civic and self-contained representation. With its restrained elegance and reference to an idealized past, Alberti's facade was thus a rhetorical trope that aimed to *persuade* its audience, rather than confront it.

At the same time, this evocation was deliberately undermined by a series of strange details that made the resurrection of antiquity a much less straightforward affair than it may have appeared at first glance. The monumental superimposition of orders that frames the stone masonry is just a thin layer of stone applied to the brick walls of the building. Rather disconcertingly, Alberti did not hide the fact that the facade was a false layer; looking closely at the masonry, one immediately realizes that it has been designed in a pattern that suggests a calculated disorder and avoids any hint of symmetry. Moreover, the design incorporated deliberate mistakes such as the absence of keystones on the window arches. The role of these details seems clear: they tempered the rhetorical role of the facade as a civic backdrop, exposing it as something fully artificial and constructed—a skillful rhetorical fiction. At the same time, these details represented the very sign of the architect's authorship. No master builder would have conceived of such trickery on a facade with the intention of expressing stability and order.

There are many questions about Alberti's authorship of this facade and the role played by the master builders who executed it. Yet his authorship is almost self-evident if we compare Palazzo Rucellai to Palazzo Piccolomini in Pienza—a building that is in many respects twinned with Palazzo Rucellai, as both were built by Bernardo Rossellino, a renowned master builder and collaborator of Alberti.[52] The facade of Palazzo Piccolomini seems identical to the one of Palazzo Rucellai but lacks the subtlety of the ambiguous details introduced by Alberti in the latter, suggesting that he had a high degree of control over its design. In the increasingly reactionary environment of the Medici's Florence, Alberti's spirit of undertaking was overwhelmingly focused on the "language games "of architecture. Yet these language games were not the architect's private business; rather, they were a device to strengthen his mastery over the building site on behalf of the patron.

Indeed the complete divorce between structure and ornament celebrated in Palazzo Rucellai manifested the separation between *designer* and *builder*, whereby the first conceives and the second executes. Beyond its rhetorical power, ornament—as a syntax informed by classical sources—became the locus of a knowledge through which the architect subordinated the builder's work, whose agency and technical expertise were in turn radically downgraded. The facade of Palazzo Rucellai is thus an extraordinary "text" in which two seemingly divergent conditions are inextricably linked: the autonomy of the architect as a *designer* and the subordination of architecture to the private interests of the patron. The rediscovery of classicism as a "public language" in the fifteenth century can therefore be ultimately understood as the rhetorical legitimization of the asymmetrical power of private interests over the public good.

Reappropriating the Project

It would take centuries before the architect's profession would be firmly established as clearly distinguished from that of the master builder. However, Alberti had set in motion a reinvention of architecture as a *project* rather than just built form. From that point on, the central problem of architecture would not be its construction, but its *design*—a word that today has become ubiquitous in many fields beyond architecture. The word *design* comes from the Latin *designare*, which means "to mark out, to devise, to choose, to designate, to appoint." As such, *design* shares the etymology of the Italian word *disegno*.

As we have seen, both Brunelleschi's and Alberti's approach to architecture were based on the priority of *disegno* over construction. In terms of built architecture, the design of a building was manifested through ornamental features such as columns, entablatures, and frames. While Brunelleschi struggled to solve the dichotomy of structure and ornament by trying to make ornament consistent with tectonics, Alberti solved the problem by separating the two while simultaneously equating ornament with architectural form. The independence of ornament from structure allowed it to *control* the visual appearance of the building, giving it a legible (though not always truthful) form through the proportions of the orders. Master builders could not determine or modify this form, as they did not typically possess the knowledge of classical sources accumulated by "architects" such as Brunelleschi and Alberti. In this way, *disegno* as *design* became a form of command over the building process, as suggested by the word itself: to design is to devise and thus to designate or appoint the person in charge. The architectural project therefore became the epistemological framework within which architecture as design—and not as mere construction—has been hypostatized in Renaissance Europe as the core of architecture itself.

It is by considering such an idea of design that we can understand the extent to which architecture as we know it today—a profession focused on the *design* of space—is profoundly embedded in the power relationships that have shaped the beginnings of modern (capitalist) society. Architecture is not just the manifestation of power relationships: its very process of production—its undertaking—through *design* implies asymmetrical power relationships. This legacy seems to foreclose a return to a "pre-project" understanding of architecture; it seems impossible to fantasize about "architecture without architects" in a world that has, from the age of colonization onward, been constructed through design.

In light of the overwhelming and problematic legacy of the architectural project, it is time to take it seriously as a crucial site of political struggle. If the idea of project-as-design has made architecture a process in which everything must be calculated in advance, we should consider reimagining "the project" in new ways. The project can be an effort of collective imagination through which we can *put forward* not just what is to be done, but what *ought to be done*. Alberti viewed the project from a deterministic perspective, relegating architectural imagination to "dreams" with no effect on the real world. In this way, he delegitimized the understanding of a project as potential—as an idea that could become reality or not—in favor of the project as mere order-to-be-executed. As with Sombart's capitalist undertaker, Alberti's project was a managerial plan that made sense only when executed: the potential was immediately consumed as an act.

However, the potential implicit in any project counters Alberti's idea of the project as an "executive" vector. An anti-Albertian idea of the project would allow the potential of ideas to exist beyond their mere execution. The recovery of the project as the manifestation of what is *potential* and not what is immediately realizable (at all costs) could make architecture not just a tool to determine our existences but also an opportunity to *interrogate* our way of living and building the world. In this sense, the project would no longer be about *how* but about *what* and *why*.

To ask *what* ought to be done and *why* is to recover precisely the *potential* nature of the project against the "spirit of undertaking"—the managerial and entrepreneurial mentality that has been dominant since Alberti. Far from being an act of undertaking driven by private interests, architecture could instead become shared public knowledge. This knowledge could transcend any form of subordination and allow all us to *think* first and eventually to build (or unbuild). Perhaps, within this idea of architecture *in potentia*, we might speak of beauty as *venustas* again, rather than as *concinnitas*. Within such a potential architecture, beauty might no longer just be the deceptive and pleasing appearance of things; it may be the truthful embodiment of justice.

Acknowledgments

Over the course of many years, several people were especially helpful in bringing this work to conclusion. First, I want to thank Jeffrey Brown, whose friendship and deep interest in architecture were a motivating factor in this book. I regret that he did not make it to the end with us. I am deeply grateful to Jeffrey and his wife and partner Elise Jaffe, who supported this project, making it possible to commission two former Yale students, Brittany Utting and Dominic Oliver Cort, to make the analytic drawings. The diagrams they painstakingly drew and redrew are as important as the text.

Matt Roman taught the Alberti seminar at Yale with me, and Pier Vittorio Aureli, Mario Carpo, and Daniel Sherer were guest speakers in the seminar. Students Carl Cornilsen and Teo Quintana transcribed all of the seminar lectures, which are the basis for my writing. Mathew Ford typed draft after draft and worked on footnotes. I tested many ideas about Alberti's built work through uncountable phone calls with Anthony Vidler and Kurt Forster, old and dear friends. And finally, I want to recognize my wife, Cynthia Davidson, who, as editor of the Writing Architecture Series, commissioned this project and took on the task of making sense of my ramblings. This book is proof that the idea of the "sole author" is untrue.—P. E.

Notes

Preface

1 Gianmarco Vergani, Peter Shinoda, and David Kesler, "Fragments of a Conversation with Jacques Derrida," *Precis* 6: "The Culture of Fragments" (1986): 49. Emphasis mine.

Chapter 1

1 Leon Battista Alberti, *On the Art of Building in Ten Books*, trans. Joseph Rykwert, Neil Leach, and Robert Tavernor (Cambridge, MA: MIT Press, 1988), 7.
2 Ibid.
3 See Robert Tavernor, "Concinnitas in the Architectural Theory and Practice of Leon Battista Alberti," PhD thesis, University of Cambridge, 1985, doi:10.17863/CAM.16319.
4 See Peter Eisenman, *Palladio Virtuel* (New Haven: Yale University Press, 2015).
5 Neil Leach in conversation with the author.
6 Rudolf Wittkower, "Alberti's Approach to Antiquity in Architecture," in *Architectural Principles in the Age of Humanism* (1949; London: Alec Tiranti, 1952), 33. First published as "Alberti's Approach to Antiquity in Architecture," *Journal of the Warburg and Courtauld Institutes* 4, nos. 1–2 (October 1940–January 1941): 5.
7 The idea of the fragment here derives from a concept in Jacques Derrida's philosophy of deconstruction, which was the focus of a conference, in 1985, on deconstruction and architecture. See Gianmarco Vergani, Peter Shinoda, and David Kesler, eds., *Precis* 6: "The Culture of Fragments" (Journal of the Columbia University Graduate School of Architecture, Planning and Preservation, 1986).

Chapter 2

The first part of this text is based on the content of a lecture presented in Peter Eisenman's seminar at the Yale School of Architecture on March 29, 2013. It also refers in part to a paper read at the conference "Texte et image. La transmission des données visuelles dans la littérature scientifique et technique de l'Antiquité à la Renaissance: pour une philologie parallèle du texte et de l'image," Institut National d'Histoire de l'Art, CNRS et L'observatoire de Paris, May 4–7, 2010, later published as "Le dessin d'architecture et le problème de la copie chez Alberti," in *Albertiana* 16 (2013): 111–121. For a more general introduction to the topic, precise citations, discussion of sources, and further bibliographical references, see Mario Carpo, *The Alphabet and the Algorithm* (Cambridge, MA: MIT Press, 2011), 51–80; *Beyond Digital: Design and Automation at the End of Modernity* (Cambridge, MA: MIT Press, 2023), 39–46; and "Alberti's Media Lab," in *Perspective, Projections and Design*, ed. Mario Carpo and Frédérique Lemerle (London: Routledge, 2007), 47–63.

1 Carpo, *The Alphabet and the Algorithm*, 54–58; Mario Carpo and Francesco Furlan, eds., *Leon Battista Alberti's*

"Delineation of the City of Rome" ("Descriptio Vrbis Romæ") (Tempe, AZ: Center for Medieval and Renaissance Texts and Studies, 2007).

2 Hartmut Wulfram, "'Scrivete i numeri in parole!' Due apostrofi dell'Alberti ai copisti nel contesto della storia del libro," *Albertiana* 16 (2013): 191–213.

3 See Nelson Goodman, *Languages of Art: An Approach to a Theory of Symbols* (Indianapolis: Bobbs-Merrill, 1968).

4 Leon Battista Alberti, *L'architettura [De re aedificatoria]*, ed. and trans. Giovanni Orlandi (Milan: Il Polifilo, 1966), I, 1.21: "erit ergo lineamentum certa constansque perscriptio concepta animo, facta lineis et angulis." Alberti, *L'art d'édifier*, trans. Pierre Caye and Françoise Choay (Paris: Seuil, 2004), 56: "le dessin est donc un projet précis et fixe, conçu par l'esprit et obtenu au moyen de lignes et d'angles." Alberti, *On the Art of Building in Ten Books*, trans. Joseph Rykwert, Neil Leach, and Robert Tavernor (Cambridge, MA: MIT Press, 1988), 7: "let lineaments be the precise and correct outline, conceived in the mind, made up of lines and angles."

5 Alberti, *L'architettura*, II, 1.95; Alberti, *On the Art of Building*, 33, here "auctor" translated as "designer."

6 Alberti, *On the Art of Building*, 33–34.

7 Carpo, *The Alphabet and the Algorithm*, 15–28, 71–80. Similar arguments, from a different point of view, have been suggested in Marvin Trachtenberg, *Building-in-Time: From Giotto to Alberti and Modern Oblivion* (New Haven: Yale University Press, 2010).

8 Vitruvius's famously obscure definition of three kinds of architectural drawings (*ichnographia, ortographia, scaenographia*, in *De architectura*, I, 2.2) seems to take some practice of architectural drawings for granted, but his own design method never refers to, and does not require, scaled drawings: see Carpo, *The Alphabet and the Algorithm*, 133–134.

9 Alberti, *De re aedificatoria*, II, 1.97: "Inter pictoris atque architecti perscriptionem hoc interest, quod ille prominentias ex tabula monstrare umbris et lineis et angulis comminutis elaborat, architectus spretis umbris prominentias istic ex fundamenti descriptione ponit, spatia vero et figuras frontis cuiusque et laterum alibi constantibus lineis atque veris angulis docet, uti qui sua velit non apparentibus putari visis, sed certis ratisque dimensionibus annotari." In Rykwert, Leach, and Tavernor's English translation the term *ratus* was not translated as "proportional" but as "according to certain calculated standards": see Alberti, *On the Art of Building*, 34. See, on the contrary, the translation and commentary in Alberti, *L'art d'édifier*, 100, n. 9, pointing out the novelty of Alberti's "proportional" drawings. Alberti's requirement of "constantes lineae" in architectural design may not refer to generic "coherent lines," as hitherto translated, but more technically to "lines with constant value throughout," meaning uniform or consistent mensural value. This would in turn suggest, again, lines that should not be perspectivally foreshortened. In his famous "Letter to Leo X" Raphael may have been the first to define the modern triad of plan, elevation, and section ("la pariete di dentro"), whereas Alberti had mentioned plans, elevations, and side views. Raphael and Baldassar Castiglione, "Letter to Leo X," ca. 1519, chap. XVIII–XXI, Archivio Privato Castiglioni, Mantua. For a recent critical edition of the text see Francesco Paolo di Teodoro, *La lettre à Léon X:*

Raphaël et Baldassar Castiglione (Paris: Editions de l'Imprimeur, 2005), 46–58. Unlike Raphael, Alberti had also stressed the role of three-dimensional models (but never as notational tools).

10 Guidobaldo Del Monte, *Planisphaeriorum universalium theoricae* (Pesaro: Girolamo Concordia, 1579), II, 58. See Filippo Camerota, "'The Eye of the Sun': Galileo and Pietro Accolti on Orthographic Projections," in Carpo and Lemerle, *Perspective, Projections and Design*, 118, n. 12.

11 See especially Branko Mitrovic, "Leon Battista Alberti and the Homogeneity of Space," *Journal of the Society of Architectural Historians* 63, no. 4 (2004): 424–439. On Poggio's rediscovery of Lucretius and the humanist revival of Epicurean atomism, see Stephen Greenblatt, *The Swerve: How the World Became Modern* (New York: W. W. Norton, 2011).

12 Today we consider the vanishing point as the perspectival representation of a geometrical point sited at infinity, but for Alberti (who does not use the term "vanishing point") the "centric point" (*centricus punctus*) is only the locus where "successive transverse quantities visually change to an *almost* infinite distance" (*paene usque ad infinitam distantiam*; emphasis mine): Alberti, *De pictura*, I, 19, in *On Painting and On Sculpture: Leon Battista Alberti*, ed. Cecil Grayson (London: Phaidon, 1972), 54–55. In Alberti's own vernacular version, the passage reads: "quali segnate linee a me dimostrino in che modo, quasi perfino in infinito, ciascuna traversa quantità segua alterandosi." Alberti, *De pictura*, in *Opere volgari*, vol. 3, ed. Cecil Grayson (Bari: Laterza, 1973), 36.

13 Piero della Francesca, *De prospectiva pingendi*, 1474–1482, MS 1576, Book 3, proposition 8, fol. 64r, Biblioteca Palatina, Parma.

14 Carpo, *The Alphabet and the Algorithm*, 135–136: The use of the expression "orthogonal projections" (or "orthographic projections") to indicate early modern plans and elevations (and/or side views or sections, as defined by Alberti and Raphael, respectively) is frequent among scholars, but is misleading as it implies a theory of parallel projections that did not exist at the time. On central and parallel, or pseudo-parallel, projections in the Renaissance, see Robin Evans's pioneering "Translations from Drawing to Building," *AA Files* 12 (1986): 3–18, republished in Evans, *Translations from Drawing to Building and Other Essays* (London: Architectural Association Publications, 1997), 154–193; see also James Ackerman's review of the latter in *Design Book Review* 41/42 (2000): 65–67; Evans, "Architectural Projections," in *Architecture and Its Image*, ed. Eve Blau and Edward Kaufman (Montreal: Canadian Centre for Architecture, 1989), 19–35; Mario Carpo and Frédérique Lemerle, "Introduction," in Carpo and Lemerle, *Perspective, Projections and Design*, 1–5; and especially Camerota, "'The Eye of the Sun,'" 115–127. The expression "orthographic projections" seems to have first occurred in François D'Auguillon (Aguilonius), *Opticorum libri sex* (Antwerp: Plantin Press, 1613), 683 (see Camerota, 118, n. 11), where however it referred to shadows projected by the direct light of the sun (unlike a physical eye, the sun could be assimilated to a geometrical point located at infinity). Indeed, with the exception of Desargues's theory of the conics (1639), which had no immediate follow-up, pre-Mongeian parallel projections were mostly discussed with regard

to astronomy and to the theory of shadows (or to artificially distorted views, such as those generated by the lenses of the telescope): see Camerota, 125. For different takes on this controversial matter, see Alberto Pérez-Gómez and Louise Pelletier, *Architectural Representation and the Perspective Hinge* (Cambridge, MA: MIT Press, 1997), and Branko Mitrovic, "Leon Battista Alberti and the Homogeneity of Space," *Journal of the Society of Architectural Historians* 63, no. 4 (2004): 424–439.

15 Raphael and Castiglione, "Letter to Leo X," ca. 1519: see di Teodoro, *La lettre à Léon X*, 46–58.

16 A similar but even stronger distinction between intuitive practice and mathematical theorization would need to apply to the history of axonometric projections, of which traces can be found in different cultures and civilizations and at different times, but of which the mathematics is entirely post-Mongeian.

17 Alberti, *L'architettura [De re aedificatoria]*, IX, 10.855.

18 Ibid., IX, 11.863.

19 Ibid., IX, 11.865: "Maxima quæque ædificatio ob vitæ hominis brevitatem et operis magnitudinem vix nunquam dabitur, ut per eundem absolvi possit, qui posuerit. At nos [standum hoc in casu censemus] auctorum destinationibus."

20 Antonio Manetti, *Vita di Filippo Brunelleschi* and *La novella del Grasso*, ed. Domenico De Robertis and Giuliano Tanturli (Milan: Il Polifilo, 1976); see p. 98: "E non vi si metteva una piccola pietra né uno mattone a suo tempo, che [Filippo] non gli volesse vedere, e se l'erano buone e se l'erano bene cotte e bene nette."

21 Carpo, *The Alphabet and the Algorithm*, 71–79, with a discussion of sources. It is not surprising that the myth of Brunelleschi as the sole inventor of the dome of the cathedral, today mostly known through Manetti's hagiographic narrative, might have been initiated by Alberti himself, who attributed the whole dome to Brunelleschi alone ("Pippo architetto") in his dedication to the same Brunelleschi of the vernacular version of his treatise on painting (*De pictura*, 1436: "struttura sí grande, erta sopra e' cieli, ampla da coprire con sua ombra tutti e' popoli toscani, fatta sanza alcuno aiuto di travamenti"). See Alberti, *De pictura*, in *Opere volgari*, 3:7–8. See also Heather A. Horton, "'Equally Unknown and Unimaginable among the Ancients': Brunelleschi's Dome and Alberti's *Lingua Toscana*," *California Italian Studies* 2, no. 2 (2011), online at http://escholarship.org/uc/item/9009k258 (consulted July 22, 2013). On the models that Brunelleschi might have built for the dome, see Massimo Scolari, "La cupola e la lanterna del Duomo di Firenze," in *Rinascimento da Brunelleschi a Michelangelo: La rappresentazione dell'architettura*, ed. Henry Millon and Vittorio Magnago Lampugnani (Milan: Bompiani, 1994; catalogue of an exhibition at Palazzo Grassi, Venice), 585c–592c and entries 261–267; and Massimo Scolari, *Oblique Drawing: A History of Anti-Perspective* (Cambridge, MA: MIT Press, 2012), 185–215.

22 Goodman, *Languages of Art*.

23 Carpo, *The Alphabet and the Algorithm*, 28–35 and 83–93.

24 Mario Carpo, "Digital Darwinism," *Log* 26 (2012): 97–105; Carpo, *The Second Digital Turn: Design beyond Intelligence* (Cambridge, MA: MIT Press, 2017), 9–55.

25 "Alberti and the Tempio Malatestiano: An Autograph Letter from Leon Battista Alberti to Matteo de' Pasti, November 18, 1454," ed. and trans. Cecil Grayson, *Albertiana* 2 (1999): 238–258.

26 Alberti, *L'architettura [De re aedificatoria]*, IX, 11.863; *On the Art of Building* (1988), 318. See Carpo, *Beyond Digital*, 173, n.12.
27 See Carpo, *Beyond Digital*, 173, n.16.
28 Frederick Winslow Taylor, *The Principles of Scientific Management* (New York: Harper, 1911), 26, 41, 59–62; Carpo, *Beyond Digital*, 42–44.

Chapter 3

1 On Tafuri's reading of Alberti, see Massimo Cacciari, "Quid Tum," *Casabella* 619–620 (1995): 168–169; Howard Burns, "Tafuri and the Renaissance," *Casabella* 619–620 (1995): 115–124; Francesco Paolo Fiore, "The Autonomy of History," *Casabella* 619–620 (1995): 102–111; Joseph Connors, "The Culture of the Fictitious," *Casabella* 619–620 (1995): 160–163; Richard Ingersoll, "Tafuri's Rome," *Design Book Review* 34 (1994): 29–31; Andrew Leach, "Manfredo Tafuri and the Age of Historical Representation," in *Walter Benjamin and Architecture*, ed. Gevork Hartoonian (London: Routledge, 2009), 9–10; Anthony Grafton, *Leon Battista Alberti: Master Builder of the Italian Renaissance* (New York: Hill and Wang, 2000), 302–315; Manuela Morresi, "Il Rinascimento di Tafuri," in *Manfredo Tafuri. Oltre la storia*, ed. Orlando Di Marino (Naples: Clean, 2009), 32ff; Andrew Leach, *Manfredo Tafuri: Choosing History* (Ghent: A&S Books, 2007); Linda Pellecchia, "Review of *Interpreting the Renaissance*," *Renaissance Quarterly* 60, no. 4 (Winter 2007): 1320–1321; Anna Giovanelli, "Il 'progetto' storico oltre il confine. Manfredo Tafuri negli Stati Uniti," in *Lo storico scellerato. Scritti su Manfredo Tafuri*, ed. Orazio Carpenzano et al. (Macerata: Quodlibet, 2019), 287–288; and the observations in the preface to my translation of Tafuri's *Ricerca del Rinascimento: Principi, città, architetti* (Turin, 1992), which appeared in English in 2006 under the title *Interpreting the Renaissance: Princes, Cities, Architects* (New Haven: Yale University Press, 2006), xvii, xx.
2 The main phases of Tafuri's reading of Alberti can be traced across a series of books and articles from 1968 to 1992, starting with *Theories and History of Architecture* of 1968, through the pivotal essay "Discordant Harmony from Alberti to Zuccari" (1979), and ending with *Ricerca del Rinascimento* (1992). As far as his pedagogy is concerned, the 1993 IUAV seminar on Alberti is also part of the last phase: "Umanesimo e architettura: Leon Battista Alberti (1404–1472) Iuav, a.a. 1992–93," in Archivio Progetti Iuav. For a list of Tafuri's courses at the IUAV, from 1968 to 1994, see Carpenzano et al., *Lo storico scellerato*, 405–406. On Tafuri's critique of, and break with, Wittkower, see, from a large bibliography, Burns, "Tafuri and the Renaissance," 115ff, and my preface to Tafuri, *Interpreting the Reanissance*, xix.
3 Rudolf Wittkower's "Alberti's Approach to Antiquity in Architecture" appeared in the *Journal of the Warburg and Courtauld Institutes* 4, no. 1–2 (October 1940–January 1941): 1–18. Only subsequently was it was incorporated (with minor changes) into *Architectural Principles* as its first chapter.
4 Here I develop arguments advanced in my essay reviewing Peter Eisenman's *Palladio Virtuel* (New Haven: Yale University Press, 2016) in *Artforum* 55, no. 3 (November 2016): 95–96.
5 Tafuri, *Interpreting the Renaissance*, 57.
6 Ibid., 16.
7 Manfredo Tafuri, *Venice and the Renaissance*, trans. Jessica Levine (Cambridge, MA: MIT Press,

1989), 128; Tafuri, *Interpreting the Renaissance*, 52.

8 Hans Blumenberg, *Paradigms for a Metaphorology*, trans. Robert Savage (Ithaca: Cornell University Press, 2016).

9 Further evidence of Tafuri's metaphorology is provided by his suggestion to take the idea of the Renaissance not in a literal sense, as an abstract "container" of various historical contents, but metaphorically, which in his view is more productive than any reified conception of this era, rooted in a traditional use of historiographical categories: see *Venice and the Renaissance*, ix–x.

10 Tafuri, *Interpreting the Renaissance*, xxix.

11 Ibid., 128. On this aspect of Tafuri's approach, see now *Architettura e storia. Un incontro polifonico con Carlo Ginzburg*, ed. Gundula Rakowitz with contributions by Daniel Sherer, Yehuda Safran, and Armando dal Fabbro (Venice: IUAV, 2024); "An Interview with Carlo Ginzburg by Yehuda Safran and Daniel Sherer," *Potlatch* 5 (2022): 1–55, esp. 19–22.

12 Antonio Foscari and Manfredo Tafuri, *L'armonia e i conflitti. La chiesa di S Maria della Vigna nella Venezia del '500* (Turin: Einaudi, 1983), 2–5.

13 Tafuri, *Venice and the Renaissance*, x–xi, 103ff.

14 Alberti, *De re aedificatoria*, IX, 5. On *finitio*, see Joan Kelley Gadol, *Leon Battista Alberti, Universal Man of the Early Renaissance* (Chicago: University of Chicago Press, 1969), 108ff.

15 Alberti appeared as an object of analysis in two early books by Tafuri, *L'architettura dell'Umanesimo* (1969) and, prior to that, *L'architettura del Manierismo nel Cinquecento europeo* (1966), both of which he disavowed, in various degrees, after 1968: see on this Burns, "Tafuri and the Renaissance," 116–117; Andrew Leach, *Crisis on Crisis: Tafuri on Mannerism* (Basel: Standpunkte, 2017). Precisely because these books occupy an ambiguous position within his output—the second in particular being repudiated by its author as an unacceptable *Jugendarbeit*—which in retrospect we may regard as that of *rites de passage* to his more mature readings of the Renaissance, I begin with his discussion of Alberti in *Theories and History of Architecture* (1968). For Tafuri's critique of the concept in his final work, see *Interpreting the Renaissance*, 13 and chapter 6. For assessments of Tafuri's early work on mannerism, see Leach, *Crisis on Crisis*; Fiore, "The Autonomy of History," 103–104; Alina Payne, *Rudolf Wittkower* (Turin: Bollati Boringhieri, 2011), 31.

16 Tafuri, *Interpreting the Renaissance*.

17 Cacciari, "Quid Tum," 169. For Tafuri's reading of the emblem, see *Interpreting the Renaissance*, 44.

18 Alberti, *De re aedificatoria*, IX, 2, 10. The second passage gives a striking connection between fame and the precariousness of the architect's work: "He [the architect] must calculate . . . the amount of praise, remuneration, thanks and even fame he will achieve, or conversely . . . what contempt and hatred he will receive, and how eloquent, how obvious, patent and lasting a testimony of his folly he will leave his fellow men." Connections with such dialogues as *De comodis litterarum et incomodis*, *Intercoenales*, *Momus*, and *Theogenius* can be traced in this passage, in which Alberti's confrontation with Stoic thought is manifest. On Alberti and the humanist conception of fame in the fifteenth century, see, from among an extensive bibliography, Jakob Burckhardt, *The Civilization of the Renaissance in Italy* (New York:

Harper, 1958), 1:149–150; Caspar Pearson, *Leon Battista Alberti: The Chameleon's Eye* (London: Reaktion Books, 2022), 117ff, and my review of this book in *JSAH* 82, no. 4 (2023): 472–473, esp. 473; Tim Anstey, "Authorship and Authority in L. B. Alberti's *De re aedificatoria*," *Nordic Association for Architectural Research* 4 (2003): 22; David Marsh, "Petrarch and Alberti," in *Renaissance Studies in Honor of Craig Hugh Smyth*, ed. Andrew Morrogh et al. (Florence: Giunti Barbera, 1985), 363–375.

19 Manfredo Tafuri, "Discordant Harmony from Alberti to Zuccari," *Architectural Design* 5–6 (1979): 36–37; cf. Tafuri, *Theories and History of Architecture*, trans. Giorgio Verrecchia (London: Granada, 1980), 15–16. On Tafuri's reading of Garin, see Grafton, *Leon Battista Alberti*, 304; Luisa Lorenza Corna, "Thinking Through Antinomies: An Enquiry into Manfredo Tafuri's Historical Method," PhD thesis, University of Leeds, 2016, 135ff; and my preface to Tafuri, *Interpreting the Renaissance*, xx and n. 33. As for Garin's contributions, see Eugenio Garin, "Il pensiero di L. B. Alberti nella cultura del Rinascimento," *Accademia Nazionale dei Lincei* 209 (1974): 28; Garin, *Portraits from the Quattrocento* (New York: Harper & Row, 1972), 120ff. On Garin, see Olivia Catanorchi, ed., *Eugenio Garin dal Rinascimento all'Illuminismo: Atti del convegno, Firenze, 6–8 marzo 2009* (Rome: Edizioni di Storia e Letteratura, 2011).

20 "In postwar Italy the literary historian Eugenio Garin," writes Joseph Connors, "described an authority-hating Alberti drenched in cynic philosophy and trapped in a world of dissimulation. This Alberti seemed a perfect match for the malaise of Italy's 'years of lead': he was seen as the skeptical philosopher, the reviver of Lucian's irony, the anticlerical cleric, the man of the permanently unhealed wound. . . . For Tafuri, a veteran of the barricades of '68, it was no longer possible to see Alberti as a collaborator with the established order." Connors, "The Lion of Florence," *New York Review of Books*, September 20, 2001, 5.

21 On the controversies surrounding Alberti's claim to authorship of this building, due to a lack of documentary evidence linking it to the architect, see Pearson, *Leon Battista Alberti*, chapter 5, and my review of this book in *JSAH*, 472–473.

22 Tafuri, "Discordant Harmony from Alberti to Zuccari," 36.

23 For an approach that stresses Alberti's attempt to coordinate the new design with the medieval structure, downplaying the conflicts involved, see Howard Burns, "Leon Battista Alberti," in Francesco Paolo Fiore, *Storia dell'architettura italiana. Il Quattrocento* (Milan: Electa, 1998), 138ff.

24 Tafuri, *Theories and History of Architecture*, 14–15.

25 Ibid.

26 Ibid.

27 In Brunelleschi's case, as has often been noted, the Gothic and classical traditions work together structurally to magnificent effect (the dome of Santa Maria del Fiore being exemplary in this regard). This is not the case in Alberti's architecture, where, instead of attaining a stable synthesis, the two idioms clash, largely at the level of representation (Santa Maria Novella, and in a different sense, the Tempio Malatestiano being the most conspicuous instances of this conflict). See, on the Gothic/classic synthesis in Brunelleschi's cupola, Giovanni Fanelli and Michele Fanelli, *Brunelleschi's Dome: Past and Present of an Architectural Masterpiece* (Florence: Mandragora,

2006). On Alberti's reception of Gothic traditions, see Franklin Toker, "Alberti's Ideal Architect: Renaissance—or Gothic?," in Morrogh et al., *Renaissance Studies in Honor of Craig Hugh Smyth*, 667–674; Pearson, *Leon Battista Alberti*, 233ff.

28 See my introduction to *Interpreting the Renaissance*, xix–xx, on this shift within Tafuri's historiographical approach.

29 Manfredo Tafuri, "Per una critica dell'ideologia architettonica," *Contropiano* 1 (1969); Tafuri, *Progetto e utopia: sviluppo capitalistico* (Bari: Laterza, 1973), translated as *Architecture and Utopia: Design and Capitalist Development*, trans. Barbara Luigia La Penta (Cambridge, MA: MIT Press, 1976).

30 This was a moment that coincided with his most important writings on Aldo Rossi, the New York Five, and the entire arc of experiences connected with the European and American neo-avant-gardes: an era marked by the unfolding of the theme of architecture's precarious autonomy. At this juncture he expressed his preference for architectures marked by "sublime uselessness" that were "pathetic in their anachronism": Tafuri, *Architecture and Utopia*, ix. On this phase of Tafuri's trajectory, see my essays "*Progetto* and *Ricerca*: Manfredo Tafuri as Critic and Historian," *Zodiac* 15 (1995): 32–51, and "Architecture in the Labyrinth: Theory and Criticism in the United States: Oppositions, Assemblage, ANY (1973–1999)," *Zodiac* 20 (1999): 36–63.

31 For the notion of "semantic crisis" (*crisi semantica*) in the visual arts, Tafuri relied on the Kantian aesthetic theorist Emilio Garroni, whose *La crisi semantica delle arti* (Rome, 1964), now almost entirely forgotten, was highly influential at the time. On Garroni, see Martino Feyles, "Technique et langage. Leroi-Gourhan, Heidegger, Garroni," in Emanuele Clarizio and Xavier Guchet, *Vie, anthropologie et politique. Perspectives italiennes contemporaines en philosophie des techniques* (Milan: Mimesis, 2019), 93–116; Cristina Coccimiglio, "Percezione e linguaggio a partire dalle riflessioni di Emilio Garroni in *Immagini, Linguaggio, Figura*," *Materiali di Estetica* 4, no. 1 (2017): 121–140.

32 Tafuri, *Theories and History of Architecture*, 187–195.

33 Erwin Panofsky, "The First Page of Giorgio Vasari's *Libro*," in Panofsky, *Meaning in the Visual Arts* (1955; Chicago: University of Chicago Press, 1984), 190–191.

34 The Tempio, however, is not the first project Alberti designed. This honor belongs to the "Arco del Cavallo" in Ferrara, a project commissioned by Leonello d'Este in 1434, using a triumphal arch as a support for an equestrian statue of his father Niccolò III, on which see Grafton, *Leon Battista Alberti*, 189–224. On this work see now Maria Teresa Sambin de Norcen, "'*Attolli super ceteros mortales*': L'arco del cavallo a Ferrara," in *Leon Battista Alberti: Architetture e committenti, Atti del Convegno internazionale del Comitato nazionale VI centenario della nascita di Leon Battista Alberti: Firenze—Rimini—Mantova, 12–16 ottobre 2004*, ed. Arturo Calzona (Florence: L. S. Olschki, 2009), 349–391. On Alberti at the Este court, see Marco Folin, "La committenza estense, l'Alberti e il palazzo di corte di Ferrara," in Calzona, *Leon Battista Alberti: Architetture e committenti*, 257–304; Grafton, *Leon Battista Alberti*, 200ff.

35 Grafton, *Leon Battista Alberti*, 316.

36 For Alberti's description of *columnae quadrangulae* see *De re aedificatoria*, VII, 15. On the sarcophagi and their setting see Grafton, *Leon Battista Alberti*, 316ff; Pearson, *Leon Battista*

Alberti, 220ff; Cecil Grayson, "L. B. Alberti, Architect," *AD* (1979): 10–13.

37 For Alberti's citation both of the proportional module and ornamental disposition of the Arch of Augustus see Rudolf Wittkower, *Architectural Principles in the Age of Humanism* (London: Warburg Institute, 1949), 37 and n. 3, who attests that in the earlier literature on the Tempio—above all, Corrado Ricci, *Il Tempio Malatestiano* (Milan/Rome: Bestetti & Tumminelli, 1924)—this reference was already an established topos.

38 Tafuri, *Interpreting the Renaissance*, 12.

39 Ibid., 18.

40 Ibid.

41 Ibid., 60.

42 Ibid., 124.

43 Ibid., 7–8.

44 Ibid., 7.

45 Ibid., 16. See also, on Alberti's impact on the Renaissance, my preface to Tafuri, *Interpreting the Renaissance*, xvii–xviii.

46 Gunter Schweikhart, "La rinascita dell'antico," in *Palladio e Verona*, ed. Paola Marini (Verona: Neri Pozza 1980), 85–102.

47 Tafuri, *Interpreting the Renaissance*, 8, 49. In the quotations in the arch of the Tempio Malatestiano at Rimini, taken from the Baptistery of Florence, as well as the ones in Santa Maria Novella's facade deriving from San Miniato al Monte and from the *sacro etrusco antico* in Sant'Andrea in Mantua, memories can be found of the *sermo* of the community where these edifices were destined to be built.

48 Cf. Angelo Turchini, "Rimini e il Tempio Malatestiano," in *Leon Battista Alberti e l'architettura. Catalogo della mostro (Mantova, 16 settembre 2006–14 gennaio 2007)*, ed. Massimo Bulgarelli (Milan: Silvana, 2006), 266–275. Grafton calls attention to the urbanistic meaning of the triumphal arch, underscored by Alberti in *De re aedificatoria*, VIII, 6, which he defined, as recognizable type, as a "gate that is continually open." In addition, since anyone entering Rimini through its main gate, on the ancient Via Flaminia, had to pass through the Arch of Augustus which Alberti cites in the Tempio, this allusion would have called attention not only to the openness of the triumphal arch typology in a general sense, but to the specific and rooted connections with the strategic and urbanistic role of Rimini in antiquity. Grafton, *Leon Battista Alberti*, 328–329.

49 Tafuri, *Interpreting the Renaissance*; Alberti, *De re aedificatoria*, VIII, 10. On Alberti's idea of the *templum etruscum*, see Richard Krautheimer, "Alberti and the Templum Etruscum," in Krautheimer, *Studies in Early Christian, Medieval and Renaissance Architecture* (New York: New York University Press, 1959), 333ff. For the reference to the Colosseum in the Palazzo Rucellai facade, a citation that can be verified by the connection of the two superior orders to the arches of the windows, see Christoph Luitpold Frommel, "Palazzo Rucellai," in Bulgarelli, *Leon Battista Alberti e l'architettura*, 344–347, esp. 347.

50 Tafuri, *Interpreting the Renaissance*, 6, 49.

51 Ibid., 49.

52 Ibid., chapter 1.

53 Aeneas Sylvius Piccolomini, *Memoirs of a Renaissance Pope: The Commentaries of Pius II*, trans. Florence A. Gregg, ed. Leona C. Gabel (New York: Putnam, 1959), 110. Curiously, this was not the first time that one of Alberti's churches was compared to a non-Christian site of worship, with distinctly negative overtones. The Mantuan church of San Sebastiano was built in an imperfectly drained swamp.

Even before the floor level was raised to protect it from rising damp it puzzled viewers, and the patron's son, Cardinal Francesco Gonzaga, professed he could not tell whether he was looking at the plans for a church, a temple, or a mosque. Franco Borsi, *Leon Battista Alberti: The Complete Works* (London: Faber, 1989), 143, with full bibliography; Connors, "The Lion of Florence," 11.

54 Grafton, *Leon Battista Alberti*, 316.

55 Burckhardt, *The Civilization of the Renaissance in Italy*, 1:235. Burckhardt emphasizes the combination of genuine learning and moral turpitude in Sigismondo, pointing out, rather drily, that even the tyrant's worst enemy, Pius II, acknowledged the learned accomplishments, and more particularly, the familiarity with ancient history, that distinguished the ruler of Rimini. This only served to drive home Burckhardt's underlying thesis, namely, that modern individuality, the will to stand out and make one's mark, for better and worse, had its beginnings in the Italian Renaissance. For Tafuri and Burckhardt, see Tafuri, *Interpreting the Renaissance*, 20, 31, and Tafuri, *Venice and the Renaissance*, ix. For a more extended analysis see my preface to *Interpreting the Renaissance*, xviii and n. 13.

56 Burckhardt, *The Civilization of the Renaissance in Italy*, 1:149–150.

57 On Alberti and Sigismondo see Angelo Turchini, "Sigismondo e Leon Battista Alberti," in Calzona, *Leon Battista Alberti: Architetture e committenti*, 407–431; Turchini, *Il Tempio Malatestiano. Sigismondo Pandolfo Malatesta e Leon Battista Alberti* (Cesena: Ponte Vecchio, 2000); Massimo Bulgarelli, "L'architettura," in *Il Tempio Malatestiano*, ed. Antonio Paolucci (Modena: F. C. Panini, 2010), 1:78ff.

58 Tafuri, *Interpreting the Renaissance*, 19.

59 Ibid.

60 Ibid.

61 Ibid., 28. "By supporting humanism and Neoplatonic culture, the learned Nicholas waged a campaign to annex mental habits that could have proven dangerous if allowed to develop autonomously."

62 See note 53 above.

63 There is no doubt that for Alberti, architecture was a kind of language: the chief evidence of this being his consistent reliance on classical rhetoric to frame his theory of architecture. See on this reliance and its wider implications Hans-Karl Lücke, "Alberti, Vitruvio e Cicerone," in *Leon Battista Alberti*, ed. Joseph Rykwert and Anne Engel (Milan: Electa, 1994), 70–95. A strong parallel can be suggested, as well, between Alberti's use of classical rhetoric in his theory of architecture and in his theory of painting: see, on this topic, Michael Baxandall, *Giotto and the Orators: Humanist Observers of Painting in Italy and the Origins of Pictorial Composition 1350–1450* (Oxford: Oxford University Press, 1971), chapter 3.

64 Alberti, *De re aedificatoria*, VI, 1.

65 Ibid. On the metaphor of Vitruvian shipwreck, see Caspar Pearson, "Between Navigation and Shipwreck: Leon Battista Alberti on the Sea of Existence," *Viator* 53, no. 2 (2023): 63–76.

66 See, for the sharp words Alberti reserves for his precursor, *De re aedificatoria* VI, 1. Recently it has been suggested that Alberti started what would eventually become his treatise on architecture as an extended commentary on Vitruvius, but found so much to object to, and so many inconsistencies in the theoretical framework of the Roman author, that he decided to make a clean

sweep and write his own treatise on partly non- or anti-Vitruvian grounds. In light of these critiques, it appears likely that Alberti's goal was to displace Vitruvius, with an entirely different standpoint and using a different set of principles. See for this intriguing hypothesis Anstey, "Authorship and Authority in L. B. Alberti's *De re aedificatoria*," 19. On Alberti's fraught relationship with Vitruvius, see Richard Krautheimer, "Alberti and Vitruvius," in Krautheimer, *Studies in Early Christian, Medieval and Renaissance Architecture*, chapter 20; Connors, "The Lion of Florence"; Pearson, *Leon Battista Alberti*, 207ff; and my talk in the Director's Seminar at the Warburg Institute, "Panofsky and Wittkower on Alberti: Divergent Receptions of *De re aedificatoria* I, 10," June 5, 2023, YouTube Warburg Institute lectures.

67 Tafuri, "Discordant Harmony from Alberti to Zuccari," 36.

68 On the problems of design and construction that compromised San Sebastiano see Pearson, *Leon Battista Alberti*, 240ff, with full bibliography.

69 Tafuri, *Theories and History of Architecture*, 16–17. Here Alberti is portrayed as a sort of ambiguous "restorer," with Tafuri following in part the contributions of Zevi and Portoghesi to this perspective; see ibid., 66, n. 12.

70 Manfredo Tafuri, "Giulio Romano: Language, Mentality, Patrons," in *Giulio Romano*, exh. cat. (Cambridge: Cambridge University Press, 1998), 11–55.

71 Tafuri, "Discordant Harmony from Alberti to Zuccari," 36.

72 Tafuri, *Interpreting the Renaissance*, chapter 2.

73 Ibid., 29–30, 31.

74 Ibid., chapter 2.

75 Ibid., 46.

76 Grafton, *Leon Battista Alberti*, 304ff.

77 Ibid., to which one should compare Leach, *Manfredo Tafuri*, 82ff; Tafuri, *Interpreting the Renaissance*, chapter 2.

78 Tafuri, *Interpreting the Renaissance*, 57.

79 Ibid.

80 G. Dehio, "Die Bauprojekte Nikolaus V. und L. B. Alberti," *Repertorium für Kunstwissenschaft* 3 (1880): 241–275. Tafuri, *Interpreting the Renaissance*, chapter 2, with bibliography, discusses the contributions of Dehio, von Pastor, Westfall, Burroughs, and other scholars.

81 Tafuri, *Interpreting the Renaissance*, chapter 2.

82 Ibid. On Porcari's rebellion, see Marta Celati, *Conspiracy Literature in Early Renaissance Italy: Historiography and Princely Ideology* (Oxford: Oxford University Press, 2021), 37–40 (on the rebellion) and72–104 (on Alberti's narration of it); Celati, "Irony, Historiography, and Political Criticism: The *Porcari coniuratione*," *Albertiana* 23, no. 2 (2020): 207–224; Massimo Miglio, "'Viva la libertà e il populo di Roma': Oratoria e politica: Stefano Porcari," in *Palaeographica diplomatica et archivistica. Studi in Onore di Giulio Batelli* (Rome: Edizioni di Storia e Letteratura, 1979), 387–421.

83 Manfredo Tafuri, "Roma Instaurata: Strategie urbane e politiche pontificie nella Roma del '500," in *Raffaello architetto*, ed. Christoph Luitpold Frommel, Stefano Ray, and Manfredo Tafuri (Milan: Electa, 1984), 59–106; Tafuri, "Via Giulia nel piano di ristrutturazione di Giulio II: un'ipotesi urbanistica e il suo fallimento (1508–1511)," in *Via Giulia. Un utopia politica del '500*, ed. Luigi Salerno, Luigi Spezzaferro, and Manfredo Tafuri (Rome: Aristide Staderini, 1975), 63–76; Tafuri, "Strategie

di sviluppo urbano nell'Italia del Rinascimento," in *D'une ville à l'autre. Structures matérielles et organisation de l'espace dans les villes européennes (XIIIe-XVIe siècle). Atti del convegno dell'Ecole française de Rome, 1–4 dicembre 1986*, ed. Jean-Claude Maire Vigueur (Rome : École française de Rome, 1989), 323–364. For a dissenting view on Tafuri's reading of Porcari, see Grafton, *Leon Battista Alberti*, 311ff. On political technology, see Michel Foucault, "The Political Technology of Individuals," in Foucault, *Power*, ed. James D. Faubion, trans. Robert Hurley et al. (New York: New Press, 2000), 403–417.

84 Tafuri, *Interpreting the Renaissance*, 35.

85 Ibid.

86 Ibid.

87 On these texts, and the theme of irony often encountered in them, see Pearson, *Leon Battista Alberti*, 194ff, and my discussion of Pearson's arguments in my review of his book in *JSAH*. On humanist irony, see Robert Klein, "La thème du fou et l'ironie humaniste," in Klein, *La forme et l'intelligible* (Paris: Gallimard, 1970), 433–450. I have been unable to consult T. Kircher, *Living Well in Renaissance Italy: The Virtues of Humanism and the Irony of Leon Battista Alberti* (Tempe: Arizona Center for Medieval and Renaissance Studies, 2012).

88 Tafuri, *Interpreting the Renaissance*, chapter 2.

89 Tafuri, "Discordant Harmony from Alberti to Zuccari," 36. Garin's theses on a "dissonant" Alberti were first put forward, to the best of my knowledge, in his *Rinascite e rivoluzioni* (Rome: Laterza, 1975), 79ff; cf. Garin, "Il pensiero di Leon Battista Alberti," *Rinascimento* 12 (1972): 3–20. On Tafuri's reception of Garin, see the brief indications in Grafton, *Leon Battista Alberti*, 304, and the indications in my preface to Tafuri, *Interpreting the Renaissance*, xx–xxi. On Garin, see F. Audisio and A. Savorelli, eds., *Eugenio Garin: Il percorso storiografico di un maestro del Novecento. Giornata di studio. Prato, Biblioteca Roncioniana, 4 maggio 2002* (Florence: Le Lettere, 2003); Michele Ciliberto, *Eugenio Garin. Un intellettuale nel Novecento* (Rome: Laterza, 2011).

90 Pearson, *Leon Battista Alberti*, chapter 4.

91 Tafuri, *Interpreting the Renaissance*, 41–43. A similar point is made from a different perspective, taking a number of literary texts of Alberti into consideration, by Pearson, *Leon Battista Alberti*, chapter 4.

92 See Alberti, *De re aedificatoria*, VII, 4.

93 Tafuri, *Interpreting the Renaissance*, 47.

94 Ibid.

95 Ibid. On the role of musical harmony in Neoplatonic speculation, see the classic study by Leo Spitzer, *Classical and Christian Ideas of World Harmony: Prolegomena to an Interpretation of the Word "Stimmung"* (Baltimore: Johns Hopkins University Press, 1945); Hans Schavernoch, *Die Harmonie der Sphären: Die Geschichte der Idee des Welteinklangs und der Seeleneinstimmung* (Freiburg: Alber, 1981).

96 Tafuri, *Interpreting the Renaissance*, 16, 47.

97 Tafuri makes it clear that he does not wish to deny the connection between mystical harmony and architecture in the Renaissance—a connection about which he sought as much precise data as possible. On the other hand, his research showed that architects were neither much interested in, nor philosophically prepared to pursue, metaphysical speculations linking concepts of harmony to their practice. See the important methodological reflections in Tafuri, *Interpreting the Renaissance*, 16.

98 Wittkower, *Architectural Principles in the Age of Humanism*, chapter 1. The emphasis on centralizing forms which Wittkower stresses in Alberti's treatise, forms which are moreover not even realized in the design he devised for Santissima Annunziata in Florence, are certainly not sufficient to make him into a bona fide Neoplatonist. Nor are the remarks on music in the famous letter to Matteo de' Pasti. On the Pythagorean substrate in Neoplatonism, see Schavernoch, *Die Harmonie der Sphären*, 33ff; E. R. Dodds, *The Greeks and the Irrational* (Berkeley: University of California Press, 1951), 143ff, 247–248.

99 For Alberti's omnivorous readings in different schools of ancient philosophy, see note 103 below; on the Pythagorean elements in Platonism and Neoplatonism, transmitted to both Augustine and Boethius, see Alberti, *De re aedificatoria*, IX, 9.

100 Alberti, *De re aedificatoria*, II, 3; I, 4; Tafuri, *Interpreting the Renaissance*, 46.

101 Tafuri, *Interpreting the Renaissance*, 46–48.

102 Ibid.

103 On Alberti's reception of Stoicism, see now Martin McLaughlin, *Leon Battista Alberti: Writer and Humanist* (Princeton: Princeton University Press, 2024), chapter 7.

104 Alberti, *De re aedificatoria*, I, 5.

105 Tafuri, *Interpreting the Renaissance*, chapter 2.

106 Tafuri, *Venice and the Renaissance*, x.

107 Tafuri, *Interpreting the Renaissance*, 20.

108 Ibid., 21. Here I further develop arguments put forward in my essay "The Architectural Project and the Historical Project: Tensions, Analogies, Discontinuities," *Log* 31 (2014): 115–138.

109 On Tafuri and Cacciari, see my preface to Tafuri, *Interpreting the Renaissance*, xx, with bibliography; my review of Leach, *Manfredo Tafuri: Choosing History*, in *Journal of Architecture* 14, no. 6 (2009): 733; Donatella Scatena, "La destruturazzione dell'ideologia architettonica. Gli anni del 'Contropiano,'" in Carpenzano et al., *Lo storico scellerato*, 349ff.

110 Tafuri, *Interpreting the Renaissance*, 50.

111 Ibid., 50–51, citing Massimo Cacciari, *Dell'inizio* (Milan: Adelphi, 1990), 359ff. In support of the nexus between *techne* and primordial guilt, Tafuri adduces the link repeatedly drawn in *Momus* between the eponymous protagonist of that dialogue and Prometheus himself: see Tafuri, *Interpreting the Renaissance*, 306, n. 116.

112 Tafuri, *Interpreting the Renaissance*, 51.

113 Ibid., 52.

114 On *concinnitas* and its origin in Ciceronian rhetorical theory, see Pearson, *Leon Battista Alberti*, 115, and my review of Pearson in *JSAH*, 473; Hans-Karl Lücke, *Alberti Index* (Munich: Prestel, 1974–1979), vol. 4, s.v. *Concinnitas*. On Alberti's reception of Cicero more generally, see, from a large bibliography, Grafton, *Leon Battista Alberti*, 12, 41, 52, 134, 168; Gadol, *Leon Battista Alberti*, 106, 156, 216.

115 On the Ciceronian meaning of the term, as compared to Vitruvian *symmetria partium*, both of which refer in different ways to a concept of inner equilibrium, see J. S. Hendrix, "Leon Battista Alberti and the Concept of Lineament," *Proceedings of University of Vienna Conference on Iconology* (2011), 6 and no. 26, online at https//docs.rwu /saahp-fp/30.

116 Tafuri, *Interpreting the Renaissance*, 46.

117 Ibid. Alberti, *De re aedificatoria*, VI, 2: "Beauty may even influence an enemy, by restraining his anger and so preventing the work from being violated." Cf. Caspar Pearson, *Humanism and the Urban World: L. B. Alberti and the Renaissance City* (University Park: Penn State University Press, 2011), 158–159; Jan Białostocki, "The Power of Beauty: A Utopian Idea of L. B. Alberti," in *Studien zur Toskanischen Kunst, Festschrift für L. H. Heydenreich*, ed. Wolfgang Lotz and Lise Lotte Möller (Munich: Prestel, 1964), 13–19.

118 Tafuri, *Interpreting the Renaissance*, 66, 67, 84, 100.

119 Alberti, *De re aedificatoria*, V, 4–5.

120 Alberti, *De re aedificatoria*; Isaiah Berlin, "The Originality of Machiavelli," in Berlin, *Against the Current* (London: Pimlico, 1979), 25–80; Garrett Mattingly, "Machiavelli's *The Prince*: Political Science or Political Satire?," *American Scholar* 27, no. 4 (Autumn 1958): 482ff. To the best of my knowledge, the first author to propose a reading of *The Prince* stressing its possibly satirical dimension was the Italian jurist Alberico Gentili, *De legationibus libri tres* (London, 1585), III, 9, 101–102.

121 Tafuri, *Interpreting the Renaissance*, 66.

122 Ibid., 64, 155.

123 Alberti, *De re aedificatoria*, VII, 5, 199. On this aspect of Albertian theory see Wittkower, *Architectural Principles in the Age of Humanism*, 38–39. On Poggio a Caiano see André Chastel, *Art et humanisme au temps de Laurent le Magnifique* (1959; Paris: Presses Universitaires de France, 1983), 18, 150–157, 218–225, 490; James S. Ackerman, *The Villa: Form and Ideology of Country Houses* (Princeton: Princeton University Press, 1990), 80–82; Per Gustaf Hamberg, "The Villa of Lorenzo il Magnifico at Poggio a Cajano and the Origin of Palladianism," in *Idea and Form: Studies in the History of Art*, ed. Nils Gösta Sandblad (Stockholm: Almqvist & Wiksell, 1959), 76–87. On the legitimacy of *licentia* in the country villa in Alberti's architectural treatise, see the succinct discussion in Veronica Biermann, "Die *'virtutes dicendi'* in Leon Battista Albertis Architekurtrakat," *Pegasus. Berliner Beiträge zum Nachleben der Antike* 11 (2009): 58 and n. 29; on the *dignitas* of the *templum*, and its position at the apex of all building types for Alberti, see Biermann, 58.

124 Alberti, *De re aedificatoria*, IX, 1–2.

125 Giorgio Vasari, "Life of Brunelleschi," in *Lives of the Artists*, trans. George Bull (London: Penguin, 1984), 1:163–164.

126 Francesco Paolo Fiore and Manfredo Tafuri, "Introduzione," in *Francesco di Giorgio architetto* (Milan: Electa, 1993), 21.

127 Frommel, Ray, and Tafuri, *Raffaello architetto*.

128 Alberti, *De re aedificatoria* I, 10. On the wall/column relationship in Alberti, see Wittkower, *Architectural Principles in the Age of Humanism*, chapter 1 (which he divides into the opposed conceptual categories of "wall and column architecture," utilizing a hypostasis that is heuristically useful yet perhaps exceeded Alberti's theoretical intentions), and Ackerman's important review of this classic and pioneering work in *Art Bulletin* 33, no. 3 (1951): 195–200, esp. 197. For further discussion see Hubert Damisch, "The Column, the Wall," in Damisch, *Noah's Ark: Essays on Architecture* (Cambridge, MA: MIT Press, 2016), 45–64, and my talk at the Warburg Institute, "Panofsky and Wittkower on Alberti."

129 Frommel, Ray, and Tafuri *Raffaello architetto*, 21. On the column as the

chief ornament of architecture in Alberti, see *De re aedificatoria* VI, 1; Veronica Biermann, *Ornamentum. Studien zum Traktat "De re aedificatoria" des Leon Battista Alberti* (Hildesheim: Olms, 1997), 134–150; Howard Burns, "'Ornamenti' and Ornamentation in Palladio's Theory and Practice," *Pegasus. Berliner Beiträge zum Nachleben der Antike* 11 (2009): 37–84.

130 Tafuri, "Giulio Romano: Language, Mentality, Patrons."

131 Tafuri, *Venice and the Renaissance*, 123.

132 Ibid.

133 Ibid.

134 On Barbaro's theoretical standpoint at the confluence of idealism and empiricism, see Daniele Barbaro, *Vitruvio, I dieci libri dell'architettura. Tradotti e commentati da Daniele Barbaro. Con un saggio di Manfredo Tafuri e uno studio di Manuela Morresi* (Milan, 1987; facsimile of the Venice edition of 1567); Manfredo Tafuri, "Daniele Barbaro e la cultura scientifica veneziana del '500," in *Cultura, scienze e tecniche nella Venezia del Cinquecento. Atti del Convegno Internazionale di Studio Giovan Battista Benedetti e il suo tempo*, ed. Antonio Manno (Venice: Istituto Veneto di Scienze, Lettere ed Arti, 1987), 55–81; Wittkower, *Architectural Principles in the Age of Humanism*, 66ff.

135 Tafuri, *Venice and the Renaissance*, 126–127.

136 Ibid., 103–138.

137 Ibid.

138 Ibid.; Foscari and Tafuri, *L'armonia e i conflitti*. On Tafuri's polycentric method as a response to and modification of Ginzburg's microhistory, see note 11 above; and my preface to Tafuri, *Interpreting the Renaissance*, xxi.

139 Manfredo Tafuri, "Committenza e tipologia nelle ville palladiane," *Bollettino del CISA Andrea Palladio* 11 (1969): 120–136; Tafuri, *Theories and History of Architecture*; Tafuri, *Venice and the Renaissance*.

140 This statement should not be taken to mean that Alberti did not have a typological concept of his own—though one that was less conspicuous, and in certain ways more closely tied to the rhetorical tradition, than Palladio's: on this aspect of Alberti, see Kurt W. Forster, "Palazzo Rucellai and Questions of Typology in the Development of Italian Renaissance Buildings," *Art Bulletin* 58, no. 1 (1976): 109–113; Biermann, "Die *'virtutes dicendi,'*" 58; C. W. Westfall, "Alberti and the Vatican Palace Type," *Journal of the Society of Architectural Historians* 332, no. 2 (May 1974): 101–121. Seeing Alberti through the lens of typology in the early 1970s was perhaps at least in part a function of the revival of interest in this concept due to the prominence attained by Aldo Rossi internationally in this period, whose Modena Cemetery dates to 1971–1972.

141 Tafuri, *Venice and the Renaissance*, 27.

142 Kurt W. Forster, "How Many Palladios Can You Count on One Hand?," keynote lecture in "What Modern Times Have Made of Palladio," Yale symposium organized by Kurt Forster with the assistance of Daniel Sherer, February 13–14, 2009.

143 Tafuri, *Interpreting the Renaissance*, 22.

144 Joseph Connors captures the motives behind such deliberate, hieroglyphic obfuscation in a reading that contextualizes Alberti's taste for paradox without diminishing its enigmatic force: "The medal also shows a strange disembodied eye borne aloft by eagle's wings, crackling with lightning like the thunderbolts

of Jove. The eye of the artist is elevated to celestial heights and made godlike. Alberti's emblem conveys his imagined self with the mystery and force of the hieroglyphs he thought he could decipher on the obelisks of Rome." Connors, "The Lion of Florence," 5.

145 Tafuri, *Interpreting the Renaissance*, xxix.

146 Ibid., 11.

147 Ibid., 22.

Chapter 4

1 See Werner Sombart, *The Quintessence of Capitalism: A Study of the History and Psychology of the Modern Business Man* (New York: E. P. Dutton, 1915).

2 Ibid., 51.

3 The undertaker must be an organizer, and organizing, Sombart wrote, "means to dovetail the work of many persons as to produce the most efficient results, so to dispose of human beings and commodities as to effect the desired creation of utilities." Ibid., 53.

4 Daniel Defoe, *An Essay upon Projects* (London: Thomas Cockerill, 1697).

5 See Marvin Trachtenberg, *Building-in-Time: From Giotto to Alberti and Modern Oblivion* (New Haven: Yale University Press, 2011).

6 Leon Battista Alberti, *The Art of Building in Ten Books*, trans. Joseph Rykwert, Neil Leach, and Robert Tavernor (Cambridge, MA: MIT Press, 1988), 313.

7 Sombart, *The Quintessence of Capitalism*, 105–109.

8 See Leon Battista Alberti, *I libri della famiglia* (Turin: Einaudi, 1994).

9 Such a mentality is inherently "projective" because, as Sombart writes, "for a perfect economy in business (and in life) you require not only thrift (which may be termed economy of matter), but also the proper coordinating of actions and the profitable employment of time (which may be termed the economy of mind)." See Sombart, *The Quintessence of Capitalism*, 56.

10 On this "side" of Alberti's work, see Mark Jarzombek, *On Leon Battista Alberti: His Literary and Aesthetic Theories* (Cambridge, MA: MIT Press, 1989).

11 Karl Marx, *Capital*, trans. Ben Fowkes (London: Penguin, 1991), 284.

12 See Trachtenberg, *Building-in-Time*; and Mario Carpo, *The Alphabet and the Algorithm* (Cambridge, MA: MIT Press, 2011).

13 For example, in his autobiography. See Leon Battista Alberti, *Autobiografia e altre opere latine* (Milan: BUR Rizzoli, 2012).

14 See Aristotle, *The Art of Rhetoric* (London: Penguin, 1992).

15 See Cicero, *On the Orator, Books I–II*, trans. H. Rackham (Cambridge: Harvard University Press, 1948).

16 John M. Najemy, *A History of Florence 1200–1575* (London: Blackwell, 2006), 273.

17 Alberti, *The Art of Building in Ten Books*, 155–156.

18 Leon Battista Alberti, *Momus*, trans. Sarah Knight (Cambridge, MA: Harvard University Press, 2003).

19 Yet ancient sources were not always easy to appropriate for the sake of legitimizing more modern and often unprecedented forms of power. In the fourteenth century, the revival of Roman law, with its emphasis on the centrality of the *populus* against the tyrannical power of rulers and aristocrats, posed a threat to monarchs and popes because it called into question the theological legitimacy of their power. See Lauro Martines, *The Social World of the Florentine Humanists 1390–1460* (Princeton: Princeton University Press, 1963).

20 On the intellectual subjectivity of the humanists, see Anthony

Grafton, *Leon Battista Alberti: Master Builder of the Italian Renaissance* (New York: Hill and Wang, 2002).

21 Trachtenberg, *Building-in-Time*, 89.

22 See chapter 2 of Grafton, *Leon Battista Alberti*.

23 Both essays have been republished in Eugenio Garin, *Leon Battista Alberti* (Pisa: Scuola Normale Superiore, 2013).

24 See Leon Battista Alberti, *Dinner Pieces, a Translation of the Intercoenales*, trans. David Marsh (London: ACMRS Publications, 1987).

25 Alberti, *Momus*, 13.

26 See Manfredo Tafuri, *Interpreting the Renaissance: Princes, Cities, Architects*, trans. Daniel Sherer (New Haven: Yale University Press, 2006).

27 Garin, *Leon Battista Alberti*, 10.

28 Chapter 2 of Tafuri, *Interpreting the Renaissance*.

29 Ibid.

30 In Herman Melville's short story "Bartleby, the Scrivener: A Story of Wall Street," first published in *Putnam's Magazine* in 1853, the titular character, a Wall Street clerk, refuses to perform various tasks by blithely intoning that he would "prefer not to."

31 See Vitruvius, *Ten Books on Architecture*, ed. Ingrid D. Rowland and Thomas Noble Howe (Cambridge, MA: Cambridge University Press, 1999). See also the fundamental interpretation of Vitruvius's theory proposed by Indra Kagis McEwen in her book *Vitruvius: Writing the Body of Architecture* (Cambridge, MA: MIT Press, 2003).

32 Leon Battista Alberti, *On the Art of Building in Ten Books*, trans. Joseph Rykwert, Neil Leach, and Robert Tavernor (Cambridge, MA: MIT Press, 1988), 154.

33 Vitruvius, *Ten Books on Architecture* [Book 4], 54–62.

34 See Alfred Sohn-Rethel, *Intellectual and Manual Labor: A Critique of Epistemology* (London: Macmillan, 1978).

35 Carpo, *The Alphabet and the Algorithm*, 71–80.

36 Alberti, *On the Art of Building*, 15.

37 Trachtenberg, *Building-in-Time*, 16–19.

38 See Alberti, *On the Art of Building*, 7.

39 Ibid.

40 Ibid.

41 See for example Giorgio Vasari, who described *disegno* as "the animating principle of all creative processes" and the "father" of all arts forms in *The Lives of the Painters, Sculptors and Architects* (New York: Knopf, 1996); originally published in 1550 and enlarged in 1568.

42 There is a famous episode narrated by Manetti in which, after returning to the building site of the Ospedale from a prolonged absence, Brunelleschi noticed the "strange" detail of an architrave folding down to run vertically along the flat columns that defined the two ends of the loggia. Such detail challenged the syntactical nature of the entablature, which is the horizontal element par excellence, and when the enraged Brunelleschi confronted the master builder who had modified the detail, the craftsman argued that this solution had been inspired by a similar feature on the Florentine Baptistery and that it therefore relied on the authority of a historical precedent. Brunelleschi rebutted that it is good to rely on examples, but that he had chosen the only wrong feature he could possibly copy from the Baptistery. This anecdote shows how the empowerment of Brunelleschi as an architect implied the downgrading of the master builder's role. Antonio di Tuccio Manetti, *The Life of Brunelleschi*, trans. Catherine Enggass (University Park: Pennsylvania State University Press, 1970).

43 Carpo, *The Alphabet and the Algorithm*.
44 See for example Rudolf Wittkower, "Alberti's Programme of the Ideal Church," in *Architectural Principles in the Age of Humanism* (New York: Norton, 1971), 3–12.
45 See Emanuele Lugli, *The Making of Measure and the Promise of Sameness* (Chicago: University of Chicago Press, 2022).
46 Alberti, *On the Art of Building*, 34.
47 Ibid., 156.
48 Ibid., 157.
49 Ibid., 156.
50 Leon Battista Alberti, "Mosca," trans. Luigi Annibaletto, in André Chastel, *Musca depicta* (Milan: Franco Maria Ricci, 1984), 43–58.
51 Massimo Bulgarelli, *Leon Battista Alberti, 1404–1472: Architettura e storia* (Milan: Electa, 2008), 25.
52 Bernardo Rossellino was also responsible for the design of Nicholas V's proposed new Saint Peter's Basilica, a project that was criticized by Alberti, as we have seen.

Contributors

Peter Eisenman is an internationally recognized architect and educator. The founder and design principal of Eisenman Architects in New York City, he is also a lifelong teacher, including twenty-two years at the Yale University School of Architecture, where he was the first Charles Gwathmey Professor in Practice. The firm's built work includes the State Farm Stadium for the Arizona Cardinals in Glendale, Arizona; the Memorial to the Murdered Jews of Europe in Berlin; the City of Culture of Galicia in Santiago de Compostela, Spain; and 6 Carlo Erba, a residential condominium in Milan. Among his many books are *The Formal Basis of Modern Architecture* (Lars Müller Publishers, 2006), *Ten Canonical Buildings, 1950–2000* (Rizzoli, 2008), *Palladio Virtuel* (Yale University Press, 2015), and *Lateness* (Princeton University Press, 2020). In 2020 he was awarded the Gold Medal for Architecture by the American Academy of Arts and Letters, an honor bestowed only once every six years, and in 2004 the Golden Lion for Lifetime Achievement at the International Architecture Biennale in Venice.

Mario Carpo is the Reyner Banham Professor of Architectural Theory and History at the Bartlett School of Architecture, University College London. Previously he was the head of the Study Centre at the Canadian Centre for Architecture in Montréal from 2002 to 2006; Vincent Scully Visiting Professor of Architectural History at the Yale School of Architecture from 2010 to 2014; Senior Scholar in Residence at the Getty Research Institute (2000–2001); Resident at the American Academy in Rome (2004); and a Guggenheim Fellow (2022–2023). His research and publications focus on the history of early modern architecture and on the theory and criticism of contemporary design and technology. His award-winning *Architecture in the Age of Printing* (MIT Press, 2001) has been translated into several languages. His most recent books are *The Alphabet and the Algorithm* (2011), *The Second Digital Turn: Design Beyond Intelligence* (2017), and *Beyond Digital: Design and Automation at the End of Modernity* (2023), all with the MIT Press.

Daniel Sherer is an architectural historian, critic, and theorist who teaches at the Princeton School of Architecture. He has taught at Columbia, Cooper Union, Cornell, Harvard, and Yale. His areas of research include Italian Renaissance and baroque architecture; modern receptions of humanist architecture; Italian modern architecture and its interactions with art and design; modern architecture and film; and historiography and theory, with an emphasis on Manfredo Tafuri. He has published widely in European and American journals including *AA Files*, *Artforum*, *Art Journal*, *Assemblage*, *Domus*, *Journal of Architecture*, *JSAH*, *Log*, *Perspecta*, *Potlatch*, *Vesper*, and *Zodiac*. He curated the exhibition "Aldo Rossi: The Architecture and Art of the Analogous City" at Princeton (2018). His translation of Manfredo Tafuri, *Interpreting the Renaissance: Princes, Cities, Architects* (Yale University Press, 2006), won the Sir Nikolaus Pevsner Book Award granted by the Royal Institute of British Architects. In 2022–2023 he was Visiting Professor at the IUAV, University of Venice, Dipartimento Cultura del Progetto. In 2025 he is Visiting Professor at the University of Ferrara, Dipartimento di Architettura.

Pier Vittorio Aureli is an architect and educator. He is a cofounder of the architectural practice Dogma, based in Brussels, and teaches at the Ecole Polytechnique Fédérale de Lausanne. He is also the author of *The Possibility of an Absolute Architecture* (MIT Press, 2011) and *Architecture and Abstraction* (MIT Press, 2023), among other books and essays.

Index

Page numbers in italic indicate illustrations.

Writing Architecture Series

1995 *Bernard Cache*, Earth Moves: The Furnishing of Territories 1995 *Kojin Karatani*, Architecture as Metaphor: Language, Number, Money 1996 *Ignasi de Solà-Morales*, Differences: Topographies of Contemporary Architecture 1997 *John Rajchman*, Constructions 1998 *John Hejduk*, Such Places as Memory: Poems 1953–1996 1998 *Roger Connah*, Welcome to The Hotel Architecture 2000 *Luis Fernández-Galiano*, Fire and Memory: On Architecture and Energy 2000 *Paul Virilio*, A Landscape of Events 2001 *Elizabeth Grosz*, Architecture from the Outside: Essays on Virtual and Real Space 2007 *Giuliana Bruno*, Public Intimacy: Architecture and the Visual Arts 2007 *Michael Cadwell*, Strange Details 2008 *Anthony Vidler*, Histories of the Immediate Present: Inventing Architectural Modernism 2009 *Léon Krier*, Drawing for Architecture 2009 *K. Michael Hays*, Architecture's Desire: Reading the Late Avant-Garde 2011 *Pier Vittorio Aureli*, The Possibility of an Absolute Architecture 2011 *Mario Carpo*, The Alphabet and the Algorithm 2012 *Massimo Scolari*, Oblique Drawing: A History of Anti-Perspective 2013 *Georges Teyssot*, A Topology of Everyday Constellations 2013 *Marco Biraghi*, Project of Crisis: Manfredo Tafuri and Contemporary Architecture 2013 *Jeffrey Kipnis*, A Question of Qualities: Essays in Architecture 2016 *Hubert Damisch*, Noah's Ark: Essays on Architecture 2017 *Mario Carpo*, The Second Digital Turn: Design Beyond Intelligence 2018 *Edward Eigen*, On Accident: Episodes in Architecture and Landscape 2021 *Andrew Witt*, Formulations: Architecture, Mathematics, Culture 2023 *Catherine Ingraham*, Architecture's Theory 2023 *Pier Vittorio Aureli*, Architecture and Abstraction 2025 *Peter Eisenman with Pier Vittorio Aureli, Mario Carpo, and Daniel Sherer*, Rewriting Alberti

Writing Architecture Series

A project of the Anyone Corporation
Cynthia Davidson, editor

The MIT Press
Massachusetts Institute of Technology
77 Massachusetts Avenue, Cambridge, MA 02139
mitpress.mit.edu

Writing Architecture Series design:
Ben Fehrman-Lee
This book was set in Lexicon by Jen Jackowitz.

This book was set in Lexicon by New Best-set Typesetters Ltd. Printed and bound in the United States of America.

Library of Congress Cataloging-in-Publication Data is available.

ISBN: 978-0-262-55371-1

10 9 8 7 6 5 4 3 2 1

Printed in Canada

EU Authorised Representative: Easy Access System Europe, Mustamäe tee 50, 10621 Tallinn, Estonia | Email: gpsr.requests@easproject.com